GRACE

IN THE FRAY

ANTICIPATING, ENDURING, AND EMBRACING LOSS

DANA ST. JOHN

Published by Dana St. John
Madras, Oregon, USA
Printed in the USA

ISBN-13: 978-1-7327678-0-5

Cover and interior design by Rob Williams, InsideOutCreativeArts.com

For additional information please e-mail Dana St. John at dstjohn@q.com.

To my three sons,
Jesse, Nathan, and Aaron,
who have walked their own journeys of grief and grace

CONTENTS

PART 1

PREPARING FOR LOSS

PART 2

PLUNGING INTO GRIEF

PREFACE

There was also a prophetess, Anna, the daughter of Penuel, of the tribe of Asher. She was very old; she had lived with her husband seven years after her marriage, and then was a widow until she was eighty-four. She never left the temple but worshiped night and day, fasting and praying.

LUKE 2:36-37

I felt sorry for Anna when I was a young woman. *What a sad life,* I thought, *to have your husband die after just seven years of marriage and then to live decades alone as a widow.* In the early days of my marriage, I had no concept that serving night and day in the temple with fasting and prayers could be a rich life of ministry and intimate communion with God. I also had no idea that I would find myself a widow at the age of forty-five and able to personally relate to Anna's situation.

Nights in the high desert of Central Oregon are often crystal clear. Thousands of stars twinkle and the Milky Way sweeps overhead. When the moon is full, moon shadows are cast across the juniper and sagebrush behind my home. A full moon often reminds me of that foggy, bitter cold December night in 1999 when my husband and his business partner's twin-engine airplane crashed into a frozen, snow-covered field miles from home. Today I still feel a quiet, lonely, melancholy connection with him as I gaze at the moon in all its fullness.

I don't think my husband lingered between life and death in that field; I hope he didn't suffer. I've wondered if in the minutes

7

before impact he knew that they were about to crash. I wonder if he thought of us in his last minutes of life. I wonder how different my life would be today if he hadn't decided to make an impromptu trip to visit a customer in Washington state that December afternoon. I think how proud he would be of his three sons who have grown into kind, responsible men of integrity. I think about all the milestones we have experienced without him; they certainly would have been more celebratory if he had been with us. I wonder what he would look like as a sixty-year-old. (I've aged, but he remains a vibrant forty-five-year-old in my mind.) I wonder what it would be like to curl up next to him on the couch, feel his coarse beard on my cheek, and just talk (I've sort of forgotten what that feels like). I wish I could share with him what I now know about myself and about God that I didn't know when he was alive. I wish he knew how significantly his spiritual walk and love for Christ have impacted me. I wish he could know how his life and death have changed me forever.

Nearly twenty years have passed since my husband's death. I have learned much over the past two decades—lessons about the undeniable sovereignty of God, His matchless wisdom, His amazing grace extended to me over and over, His unconditional love, the infinite riches available to me in Christ, and the reality that He will eventually bring restoration and make all things new. I have learned that there is purpose to life both with and without my husband by my side. I have learned that loss is universal and that if you haven't yet experienced significant loss in your life, you most likely will before you breathe your final breath. I have learned that we need to care for those around us who have experienced deep loss. I have learned that pain can refine the human soul. And I have learned that God is not finished refining or restoring any of us yet.

This book is not a handbook providing clinical explanations of grief or a twelve-step plan on how to walk through loss.

Neither is it an autobiographical recounting of my twenty-two years with a wonderful husband and dedicated father or the story of my husband's sudden death and my floundering to parent our three sons solo—although elements of my story are traced throughout its pages. This book is a picture of God's grace reaching down with a firm but tender hand to grow my trust and faith in Him while in the middle of my emotional and spiritual fray. It is about my experience of finding God's grace and mercy in the depths of crisis.

God used the death of my best friend and lover to teach me intimate truths about myself but also, more importantly, about Himself—truths I couldn't have learned aside from my pain, suffering, and brokenness. I am a better woman because I'm a widow than I would have been otherwise. Through intense, penetrating sorrow, God has taught me deep lessons and grown in me the unshakable assurance that He has everything under control (even when I can't make sense of what He is doing) and that His loving purpose can transform something terrible into something wonderful.

The lessons I have learned over the last twenty or so years are lessons any believer in Christ could discover; I just happened to face them full on in the context of widowhood. They are not new or original revelations but principles the Holy Spirit used to refine me. They have, however, profoundly changed my relationship with Christ and deeply impacted my daily walk.

I found some of my encouragement and resolution to write my story in Psalm 107:2, which instructs those who are redeemed to "tell their story." Psalm 78:4–7 also prodded me to collect in one place the lessons I had learned and lived so that eventually I could share them with my sons, daughters-in-law, and grandchildren: "We will tell the next generation the praiseworthy deeds of the LORD, his power, and the wonders he has done . . . which he commanded our ancestors to teach their children, so the next generation would know them, even the children yet to be born, and they in turn would tell their children. Then they would put their trust in God and would not forget his deeds but would keep his commands."

This book, besides being for my family, is for those who come behind me—any woman, whether single or married or mothering children, who seeks the fullness of life in Christ in this world of uncertainty in which we live. It is for those who long to live each day resting securely confident in God's love, wisdom, and sovereignty. We are not guaranteed carefree, blissful days because we follow Christ. Quite the opposite; Jesus said that we should anticipate, even expect, loss, suffering, sorrow, and pain. My hope is that those who come after me will be encouraged to face the reality that loss of various kinds are part of life in this broken world and that by understanding and accepting this, they can gain wisdom that will make today and all their tomorrows fruitful and full. Thus they will build up treasure for days ahead, when loss will in some shape or form become their own experience, and ultimately when they see God face to face in heaven.

In many ways my first few years of widowhood truly were a battle. I didn't realize that I was in a spiritual skirmish at the time and that in the midst of my loss and sorrow, the battle was not of flesh and blood but in the heavenly realms (see Eph. 6:12). But as I learned to fight, I discovered that the stark reality of my loss didn't necessitate a bleak future—a sobering future, yes, but certainly not one without hope and purpose. It is my desire to share with you in this book some of the lessons God has patiently taught (and continues to teach) me through my journey as a widow. I hope to encourage and challenge you to make the most of the season of life in which you find yourself. We have kingdom work to do. We have more lessons to learn. We have more battles to fight. We have a purpose to fulfill in this time and this place. In it all we can find God's grace in the midst of the fray.

AKNOWLEDGMENTS

We never know how impactful sincere encouragement can be to another person. My genuine gratitude goes to Gerald and Judy Webb, Peter Wierenga, and Julie Cox, who, quite independently of one another, all encouraged me to write. Corporately, their nudges gave me the courage to undertake the challenge of organizing my thoughts and getting them down on paper. Thank you so much for prodding me to step outside my normal routine and take a stab at writing.

My special thanks to my daughter-in-law Angelica, who spent hours with me when this manuscript was in its infancy and needed lots of massaging, reworking, and reorganizing. She connected me to Becky Lawson, who patiently held my hand through the editing and publishing process and provided invaluable insight. Becky then directed me to a gifted graphics guy, Rob Williams, and a talented proofreader, Jennifer Cullis. All played significant roles in turning my vision for this book into reality.

My sons deserve more than just my gratitude; they deserve medals for enduring months of tears and unpredictability during the years immediately surrounding the death of their dad. They deserve kudos for earnestly (albeit sometimes awkwardly) trying to comfort their mom when they were also struggling in their own pain. All three of them gave me purpose to continue functioning "normally" during that long season of confusion and grief.

I'm grateful for my parents and siblings, who invested hours with me on the phone after Roger's death, much of the time just listening. Their support over the long haul has been integral in helping to fill the gaping hole in the fabric of our family left by Roger's death.

I am thankful to Glenn Johnson, Roger's and my first pastor as a married couple. He continued to shepherd us long after we moved from Spokane and left his flock. Then he sought me out when I was a young widow who lived hundreds of miles from him and multiple times spoke words of comfort and encouragement to me. "Once your pastor, always your pastor," he told me.

A salute of gratitude goes to Dave Budden, who faithfully lowered the company flag to half mast every December 22 in honor of his bosses. I am thankful to him for remembering our loss publicly. That meant more to me than he will know.

I'm deeply grateful to my longtime friend Vicki Anderson, who didn't quit being my friend when I was grieving, depressed, grumpy, despondent, unloving, and downright prickly. She has exemplified Proverbs 17:17. I am thankful to her especially for including all of us in her family's holiday dinners over the past two decades.

I am thankful for the body of Christ in Madras. Even though our family had been in town for only six years when Roger was killed, the church body embraced us with love, practical help, advice, food, and more food. I will never know all the people who prayed for the St. John family over the years, but I am truly grateful for their obedience to "bear one another's burdens."

Finally, all thanks to Him who gave everything that I might be redeemed, transformed, and empowered to live above my circumstances. If it wasn't for the hope of eternal life He offers, the love He expresses, the comfort He gives, and the ability He has to restore the broken, I would have nothing to write about.

Candid Conversation

When was the last time you had a substantive conversation on the topic of grief or loss? Unless you have experienced a profound loss, you probably haven't had one. Seriously, who elects to dwell on sorrow, loss, or death, let alone talk about it? You're not likely to have listened to a podcast or heard a radio program on the topic either. Loss may not even be a frequent sermon topic in the church you attend. And while one can find scores of books and articles written on topics such as widowhood, the loss of a child, or some life tragedy, the propensity of these writings is frequently to recount a personal story and the events surrounding the loss rather than focus on biblical lessons learned through the experience.

Having been without my husband for almost twenty years now, I can count on one hand the number of times I've been asked what God has done in my life through these transformative years since his death. Certainly twenty years ago, my forty-something peers did not bring up the topic of widowhood when I was struggling without my husband, maybe not surprisingly. Yet very few women of any age over the years have asked me about my personal insights or perspective regarding what God has taught me over my years as a widow. (Maybe that says more about me than them!)

The sobering reality, however, is that most married women will be a widow someday. The US Census Bureau estimates that 975,000 American women will become widows in the next calendar year.[1] About 11.64 million widows live in the United States today.[2] Women generally outlive men, so the fact that widows outnumber widowers in the United States four to one[3] isn't surprising. If you are a married woman, there is a good probability you will live some portion of your life as a widow.

Significant loss, however, isn't unique to the woman whose husband precedes her in death. In 2016, nearly forty-five thousand Americans died by suicide.[4] That represents forty-five thousand families who struggled through their grief with complicated emotions and often unanswered questions. More than thirty-two thousand people are killed and two million injured each year from motor-vehicle crashes.[5] If thirty-two thousand people die, think of all the people who loved those individuals and are grieving. Suffering people are all around us. We assume that parents won't bury their children, but according to the Centers for Disease Control and Prevention, the infant mortality rate in the United States is 5.9 deaths per one thousand live births.[6] When one child dies, two parents sorrow.

Besides the "life will never be the same again" loss experienced through death, our days are filled with a myriad of other types of heartbreaking loss. Grief is not reserved for loss through physical death only. All losses are a kind of death in their own right. Suffering and confusion come through the loss of a dream, loss of finances, loss of health, loss of marital love, loss of friendships, loss of purpose. Who among us has not known the confusion and pain of such grief? Repeatedly throughout our lives we encounter suffering, loss, and death. And all around us others are struggling with their own losses. We live in a world tainted by sin, so of course there will be suffering, and life will be filled with "thorns and thistles" (Gen. 3:18) and death. It will eventually touch each of us. We should not assume that we will be immune from loss.

We don't like to think about loss and death. Western society puts a lot of energy and money into perpetuating the lie that we can beat the odds and stay young and extend life on and on. The message of Christianity also has been twisted by some to make us believe the false assumption that faith in Christ equals material prosperity, convenience, and life on our own terms. We have removed ourselves from close contact with disappointment and bereavement and neglected serious examination of what the Bible says about loss and sadness. In many ways we have become death deniers.

Distancing ourselves from the reality of loss and death, interestingly, is unique to this last century. Historically, death and its inevitability were seen as motivators to make the most of this life, to live meaningful and virtuous lives. As long ago as the Roman Empire, a tradition of *memento mori* (Latin for "remember that you will die") was evidenced in Western antiquity's art and architecture. The art displayed in churches, on building facades, and even in homes compelled viewers to reflect on the brevity of life and dedicate themselves to prepare to meet God.

If this section of the introduction were an Old Testament psalm, I might insert the instruction *selah* right here. Some scholars have interpreted *selah* to mean that readers should pause, step back from the text for a moment, and think about what they have just read.[7] *Selah* encourages the reader to engage with the text and consider its implications. Pause and think about this: You will die. Your husband will die. You may lose a parent or a child or face a terminal illness. In short, you will suffer loss; you will experience heartache and sorrow. What might that look like for you? How might you handle major loss and grief? Could you do some things today to prepare for life without your loved ones in the future? Have you talked with those you love about the inevitability of suffering, loss, and dying?

Death, loss, and grief are significant topics that need to be discussed in light of who God is and what He has promised us. Because "God upholds heaven and earth and all creatures, and so governs them that leaf and blade, rain and drought, fruitful and barren years, food and drink, health and sickness, riches and poverty, indeed, all things, come not by chance but by His fatherly hand,"[8] therefore we can know that loss also comes by His fatherly hand. We don't plunge into seasons of grief by accident (even when the death of a loved one is by an accident).

Suffering does not make for comfortable conversation in our culture. Yet all of us will come face to face with it at some point in our lives. Maybe it's time for the awkward silence to shift to candid conversations.

The Analogy

The final shove to motivate me to begin writing came from an impromptu raft trip I took on the lower Deschutes River in Central Oregon—certainly an unlikely persuader, but God is not bound by standard operating procedures to nudge His children to obey His promptings. God used a summer rafting experience with a group of strangers to give me fresh insight into my years as a widow and plant the idea of this book in my heart.

Jesus often taught substantial truths through parables and analogies; it was a powerful way for His hearers to grasp big ideas and remember the message. One afternoon of river rafting provided me with a great analogy of the three distinct life stages I have experienced as an adult woman: my years of being a wife and mother, my season of grief, and my later assignment of living the abundant life as a widow. These stages of my life correlated to three distinct sections of the river trip.

The first section of the river, where my co-rafters and I put in the raft, had relatively flat water. As we began our journey down-river, I saw a few riffles and areas of fast current, but for the most part it was a lovely float on a summer day. This initial part of the trip reminded me of my twenty-two years of marriage. As a family, we loved one another and enjoyed our life together. We encountered rough spots along the way, of course, and we had our share of challenges, but overall life was rewarding and full. Typically this is the longest season of a married woman's life, although certainly we have no assurances of its longevity. In this season of my life, God's grace was lavished on me as I unknowingly approached widowhood.

About midway through my raft trip, we encountered the only class IV set of rapids of our trip. A class IV rapid is described by the international scale of river difficulty as "intense, powerful but predictable rapids requiring precise boat handling in turbulent water. Depending on the character of the river, it may feature large, unavoidable waves and holes or constricted passages demanding fast maneuvers under pressure."[9] This is an extraordinary description of grief—"intense," "powerful," "unpredictable," and "unavoidable passages." It certainly described my initial years of widowhood. These years constituted for me a period of life of just trying to stay in the boat. They were overwhelming and disorienting. They were painful and lonely. During these two or three years, I functioned out of survival mode, yet I also experienced God's grace as I groped to survive as a new widow.

The final section of the river that day was a combination of fast water, wonderful scenery, and sandy beaches, all while being soaked to the skin. These last few miles were quite different from the frothing white water of the rapids. I wasn't the same, either, after having gone through the white water. (For starters, my wet clothes were visible evidence of my plunge through the rapids.) Some anxiety was behind me; I had survived the rapids. I felt a sense of accomplishment. I lifted my eyes to take in a long view of the river ahead and found new energy to conquer the rest of the adventure. This is the season in life in which today I find fulfillment and contentment in the time and place God has assigned me. I am not the same person I was before the death of my husband; I have been marked and matured by the experience. Daily I see God's grace extended to me as a widow who is precious to Him.

At the end of my day of rafting, we loaded all the gear onto a trailer and climbed onto the shuttle that would take us back to our vehicles. The road we drove down paralleled the Deschutes River. From that vantage point, fifteen to twenty feet above the water, I watched other summer rafters negotiating the rapids. The rapids didn't look all that daunting from the safety of the vehicle. However, having just been on the river, I knew what it felt like to be engulfed by the roaring water.

Life as a woman is a lot like negotiating those rapids. But through all life's seasons we can be assured of God's love, His presence, and His ability to orchestrate every detail of our journeys. He is ever in control, and the powers of death and darkness cannot thwart His plan (see Job 42:2). No matter the circumstances, God does not forsake His children (see Neh. 9:19), and because of who God is, we can experience His grace even in our storms.

Honest Talk

So biblical conversations on the topic of loss and grief are crucial and need to be candid. It's not a comfortable topic. But discussing death is not disheartening, because God who is in control of all that comes into our lives has promised that nothing can separate us from His love—"neither death nor life" (Rom. 8:38). It isn't depressing, because God promises to reveal Himself strong in our lives when we are at our weakest (see 2 Cor. 12:9; Heb. 11:34). It isn't morbid, because God ordained all the days that were prepared for us before one of them came to be (see Ps. 139:16), so an untimely death is not an indication that God is not in control. It isn't funereal, because those who are in Christ have hope—hope for today and eternal hope (see Heb. 6:17–19).

As followers of Christ, too often we have neglected to prepare for the possibility of tragic loss. We need to probe our hearts and ask if we have made marriage or family a qualification for a happy and meaningful life. Do we think of ourselves or others as less significant if we or they are unmarried? Have we avoided discussing the possibility of the death of a spouse, fearful that merely mentioning it will be a jinx? Have we intentionally or unintentionally denied the likelihood of suffering in an effort to limit our own discomfort? And have we come to so highly value the temporal and material blessings of this world that we have forgotten where our real home is?

Honest thinking and talking about these hard issues will result in several things.

First, it will enable us to offer support and walk through the dark days of grieving with others who have suffered loss. To do this we must intentionally study and reflect on God's Word so we can address the topic of loss and grief biblically. A lack of attentive consideration to this difficult discussion now may mean we won't do a healthful job of being there for a grieving friend.

Second, candid biblical conversation about these difficult matters will also prepare us personally for potential future loss, when a personal sustaining faith that holds solid during the dark days of grieving requires intentional effort. If we neglect to prepare for the possibility of pain and suffering, our loss will be more devastating than it would have been otherwise.

Finally, it will open our eyes to the unique ministry opportunities available to us because we have suffered a great loss and been matured and refined. Our culture does a pitiful job of communicating a vision for impactful service for the brokenhearted and weak. We could learn a lot from the prophetess Anna on this subject. When we understand that our value goes beyond our role as wives and moms and extends to powerful service in God's kingdom, then we can find beautiful purpose in the years after grief and loss.

If you are in a joyful season of marriage, family, or peaceful blessing, may you find encouragement and be challenged to be proactive in deepening your relationship with God today in preparation for the possibility of future loss. If you are in a season of fresh grief, I pray that you will find comfort and courage as you walk through these long days of bleakness. And if you are a seasoned veteran of loss or suffering, I trust that you will be energized and mobilized not to waste your unique calling during these years of your life. In all cases, we should strive to live each day with confidence, not in ourselves but in God, "who is able to do far more abundantly beyond all that we ask or think" (Eph. 3:20, NASB).

Most likely I've been a widow longer than most will be. Walking through life without my husband for multiple years has given me firsthand insights that I might not have acquired in just a few years of widowhood. My hope is that this book will shed light on some of our culture's misconceptions about bereavement, dashed dreams, and loss, and start intentional conversations around the topic of what biblical loss should look like.

PART 1

Preparing for Loss

Make every effort to add to your faith goodness; and to goodness, knowledge;
and to knowledge, self-control; and to self-control, perseverance;
and to perseverance, godliness.

2 PETER 1:5-6

Grow in the grace and knowledge of our Lord and Savior Jesus Christ.

2 PETER 3:18

1

The House on the Rock

Before witnesses on a hot August day in 1977, I said the words "till death do us part" to my soon-to-be husband. Like most brides, I dutifully repeated the words my pastor told me to say, but I was too nervous to really consider the words coming off my lips. I can assure you, I didn't think about the death of my husband on my wedding day. (Actually, it's sort of creepy and a bit twisted to even talk about.)

A couple years later, as I attended the wedding of a college friend, I heard the words with new ears. The bluntness of the phrase "till death do us part" hit me: this commitment was until I died or he died! Someday one of us (and statistically most likely I) would be alone. Those words hadn't been inserted in my friend's or my own wedding vows to instill fear or cast a shadow of gloom over our wedding days but to be reminders of the seriousness of the marriage covenant we were making—and of the brevity of life. The foundational marriage principle we were agreeing to was not to terminate our marriage. We were also acknowledging that God in His love and wisdom would sovereignly determine when our earthly union would come to its end. That was God's right, and He exercised His authority in my marriage much sooner than I ever anticipated He would.

Over the years since my husband's death, I've wondered if I could have done anything during my married years to lessen the trauma of my grief when I was engulfed in pain and sorrow due to sudden widowhood. Should I have been more dedicated spiritually? Should I have loved God more or my husband less? Should I have been taking additional spiritual-development steps? Could I have done something more to strengthen my faith and thus lessened the pain of my loss? Was my view of God skewed? Was it even possible to prepare for a future devastating loss?

I did not entertain these thoughts in any significant way while my husband was alive, but they have gnawed at me since his death. Today I'm a huge proponent of the necessity of wrestling through difficult theological and spiritual questions. I encourage and applaud serious grappling with the difficult aspects of the Christian faith rather than lazily accepting canned Sunday school answers. My own exercise of asking hard questions has solidified my personal convictions and redoubled my faith. It has also exposed genuine weaknesses in my walk with Christ. I discovered significant chinks in my spiritual armor that I needed to address. At times I have even been unrealistically critical of my past spiritual walk. It has been my perpetual struggle to find a healthy biblical balancing point between the extremes of recognizing my weaknesses and strengthening and reinforcing my faith.

I don't share my questionings and faith struggles here (I've offered only a short list here, mind you!) to bemoan what might have been but rather to provide insight and encouragement for those who come behind me. God tells us through the prophet Jeremiah that He welcomes those who earnestly seek Him: "You will call on me and come and pray to me, and I will listen to you. You will seek me and find me when you seek me with all your heart" (Jer. 29:12–13). God patiently offers us second, third, fourth chances to grow in grace and knowledge of Him. He's not finished with me (or you) yet.

So back to the question: is it possible to spiritually prepare for significant loss, including the death of a family member or spouse? I think the answer is yes. I base that conclusion on my own experience but also on years of observing how other Christians have responded to the deaths of those they dearly loved or to some other momentous crisis over the long haul. Some struggle with their loss, grieve, and in due season regain spiritual equilibrium, finding purpose and direction in life. Others flounder in their faith, withdraw, see themselves as victims, and seemingly never really recover. What makes the difference?

Through an analogy of two builders, Jesus taught His followers about building their spiritual lives on a solid foundation—and doing that building before the season of testing was upon them (see Matt. 7:24–27).

One builder, who understood the importance of a house's foundation being anchored to something that would not move, even in the midst of a storm, chose a solid rock upon which to build. The Greek word used by Jesus for the kind of rock the building was anchored upon was *petra*. This refers to a mass of rock as opposed to a detached stone that could be thrown or a boulder that could be moved. The builder started construction of his home before the storm approached, so when the rains came and the winds blew and the rivers of water (the rapids that lay ahead in life) burst against his house, it did not fall, because its foundation was on the *petra*.

In contrast, the foolish builder decided to build his house on the sand. No doubt it was easier building, but sand doesn't provide a substantial foundation upon which to anchor a structure. When the storm engulfed his house, the structure was not able to withstand the force of the rain and wind. Jesus said, "It fell—and great was its fall" (Matt. 7:27, NASB). Neither the foolish builder's preparation nor his construction strategy was adequate for the storms his house was eventually exposed to.

The wise woman can learn a lot from the analogy of the two builders in her early years, which for many are relatively peaceful and happy and show no evidence of an approaching storm. These years can be a significant season in which to begin the spiritual equipping for what lies ahead.

Can certain pre-loss principles result in a predictable outcome? No. It would be presumptuous to function under the assumption that a particular formula will ensure any outcome. The path of our futures is God's realm. But certain biblical principles, when applied, will feed our souls, give us hope, and strengthen our faith.

No doubt spiritual preparation for the likely eventuality of loss will be different for every woman. Yet four prevalent principles, which we will consider in the following four chapters, can bring any woman closer to significant spiritual preparedness: knowing God, cooperating with His arranging of our lives, thinking rightly about Him, and being grateful to Him. God obviously knows what each of us will be facing this afternoon, tomorrow, next week. Ultimately, preparation for the future is dependent upon Him who shapes our days and brings experiences into our lives to refine us. God plays the leading role in our preparation. But I am also persuaded that the believer has the responsibility to "work out [her] salvation" (Phil. 2:12). That burden of responsibility is not to earn salvation but to actualize it, or make it real. The actualization process authenticates faith, and authentic faith is like the house built on the rock—when the winds blow and the rains pelt against the house, it stands.

God used my twenty-two years of marriage as a tool to refine, mold, and equip me for the days He ordained for me here on Earth (see Ps. 90:12) and for eternity. During my years with my husband, I couldn't know the ways in which God was using my marriage to equip me for widowhood. Now with all the wisdom of hindsight, it is ironic to see that marriage was a significant training ground for my life without my husband.

2

Welcome the Guide

The most critical and revolutionary preparation for any kind of loss is to know Jesus Christ as our guide. I cannot imagine how I would have navigated marriage or widowhood without knowing God's grace through His Son, Jesus Christ.

When it comes to rafting, I could accurately be described as a neophyte. My rafting adventure actually started on a bit of a whim. Without a lot of advance planning, I decided to do a half-day raft trip. This was definitely outside my normal Saturday activities. I understood enough to realize, however, that if I was going to get in a raft that would soon be moving rapidly downriver, I would need a guide in the raft with me.

I wanted the assurance that someone would be in charge who knew the twists and turns of the river, knew how to handle the raft in the rapids, had all the necessary gear, and had a good track record of returning all the rafters back to shore at the end of the day. The only way I would get into an eight-man inflatable rubber raft to venture into surging white water was with the assurance that an experienced guide would be there with me—emphasis on *experienced*. Indeed, other people would be in the raft, but they could be equally as inept as I, so I couldn't count on them for any significant help if help would be needed.

With a sense of relief, I learned that the guide assigned to my raft had been taking novices down the Deschutes River every summer for twenty-two years. My river guide had a keen knowledge of the river and was aware of what lay ahead. He also knew the skill set (or lack thereof) of his crew. I found comfort in his past history and his genuine enthusiasm for the day's river trip. The humble confidence he exuded as those of us assigned to his raft gathered by the river's edge was contagious.

Salvation through Christ, more than any other thing, equipped me for all the trials, sadness, and pain I would face.

Christ extended His grace to me when I was a teenager. Receiving God's grace, His undeserved favor, meant that I got what I needed but didn't deserve. His grace rescued me from me. Because of my wrongdoings, offenses, deficiencies, faults, shortcomings—all the rebellious things that exposed my ugly nature— I didn't deserve salvation. My sin created a gaping chasm between God and me. However, because of His perfection, Christ was able to bridge the void that separated me from God. When God became man in the person of Jesus Christ, He physically walked alongside humanity (see John 1:14). He left His heavenly throne and kingly crown to become man.

It was not just because mankind required some assistance to cope with the fleeting years of our earthly existence but because we were all broken and without hope. We had all gone astray (see Isa. 53:6). We were all lost. "It is by grace you have been saved, through faith—and this not from yourselves, it is the gift of God—not by works, so that no one can boast" (Eph. 2:8-9). Grace freely given made it possible for me to have Christ as my rescuer and guide.

I don't want to give the impression that Jesus is *only* my life guide, someone I take along as insurance or to make my temporal existence here on Earth safe, comfortable, fun, and convenient. Through His substitutionary death in which He stepped in and paid what I owed for my sins, He accomplished much more for me than merely smoothing out life's rough spots. My desperate need for a Savior to rescue me *from* God's wrath was only part of what Christ did for me. He also freed me *for* something—something bigger than myself.

I did need the Guide to accompany me through the ragged moments of life and point me in the right direction, but I also needed an understanding of who I was and why I had been created. In Christ I found both my identity as His child and my purpose as His follower—both of which sustained me in the days and years following the loss of my husband. Christ envisioned a grander goal for my life than I ever could have imagined, and He masterfully used my daily responsibilities and pressures to move me along the path for which I had been saved. Through challenges, trials, pain, delays, and suffering, He expertly used each circumstance He allowed to touch my life to equip me for His purpose, His glory, and my good. Taking Him as my guide prepared me for my years of widowhood in a way nothing else could have, giving me hope and purpose when all seemed lost.

3

Cooperate with the Guide

Taking Jesus as our guide is key to building a strong foundation in our lives. But Jesus does more than walk ahead of us as our guide. He has also gone before us, preparing the way for our futures before we could have ever known it. God has worked in advance to ensure that our journeys are successful, purposeful, and, most importantly, spiritually fruitful. When we recognize that He has actually orchestrated our daily circumstances to shape us for the inevitable trials to come, we can better realize His loving hand in our lives and cooperate with Him in what He's doing.

Before I even made reservations for my rafting adventure, my guide was already preparing for our trip. He inspected our life jackets, repaired equipment, provided dry bags to hold our gear, stocked the first-aid kit, and took care of many other details, most of which I was oblivious to. He even packed squirt guns for anticipated water wars with the "rival" raft companies expected to be on the river the same day. He had gone before me by anticipating the physical things our group would need to ensure a successful and enjoyable journey down the river. Gradually realizing much of what he'd done as we journeyed down the river increased my confidence in him.

God as my guide also wisely and lovingly went before me during my married years but in a different way from my river guide. God's provisions for my journey weren't for my physical comfort and convenience; He provided instead for my spiritual development. It wasn't that God didn't care about my creature comforts—He did. His higher priority, however, was my spiritual growth. He intentionally went before me, orchestrating the details of my life in order to equip me to pass the faith tests I would encounter.

During my marriage, God used routine things to equip me for what I would face in the future. For a period of about four years, my husband's job required him to travel a lot when two of our sons were young. Out of necessity I took on household tasks that normally he would have taken care of—tasks like dealing with the finicky smoke alarm, jumpstarting the car after a little person had left the glove box open all night and that tiny light inside had drained the battery, dealing with the dead rodent in the crawl space of the house, gingerly escorting the baby skunk out of the yard, and parenting alone.

During those years I often felt isolated and longed for adult conversation. I viewed many aspects of having a husband who traveled as a hardship. But God was not surprised by any of the challenges I faced. Quite the opposite—He had orchestrated these events to prepare me for the future. I can see God's hand all over those petty inconveniences and frustrating challenges; they were expressions of His infinite love and wisdom, and evidence of His unique preparation for the days when truly I would parent alone.

God also used the myriad of Bible studies I participated in and led over the years when I was married to mature me and prepare my path. The benefits of investing in God's Word were immediate, of course, but they also served as preparation for future days.

One study in particular equipped me. It was a small-group Bible study that focused on memorizing a verse of Scripture each week. Those verses, hidden away in my heart years ago, have flooded back into my thoughts hundreds of times since then. They are genuine treasures in my spiritual portfolio. Chuck Swindoll wrote, "I know of no other single practice in the Christian life more rewarding, practically speaking, than memorizing Scripture. . . . No other single exercise pays greater spiritual dividends! Your prayer life will be strengthened. . . . Your attitudes and outlook will begin to change. Your mind will become alert and observant. Your confidence and assurance will be enhanced. Your faith will be solidified."[1] God used the personal discipline of Bible memorization to establish in me the unshakeable faith foundation He knew I would need.

Over our twenty-two-year marriage, my husband and I lived in five different towns in two states. There's nothing like relocating to a new city to push the lonely believer back into close communion with God. Every move was a time of accelerated spiritual growth for me. Each move reminded me of my dependence upon God to provide for my spiritual and relational needs and those of my husband and children. Uprooting our family, leaving wonderful friends behind, being drawn to God in a new community were strategic parts of His refining grace. God was giving me what I needed, not necessarily what I wanted: His grace.

Frequently the opportunities God provided to mature me looked a lot like trials, responsibilities, interruptions, hardships, sorrows, setbacks, and losses. But truthfully they were the faith-building exercises I needed to gain perseverance, maturity (see James 1:3-4), and godliness—all attributes I would come to depend on for what was around the next bend in the river. Christ as my guide not only knew the way ahead, but He also knew me. God's plans for my life were (and are) grander than I had envisioned.

God uniquely prepares us for our futures. He takes the lead, wisely and graciously providing for us and instructing us so that what He is teaching us today will be the exact equipping we will need for tomorrow. The woman who trusts God's hand in her life will partner with God in the preparatory work He is doing. There is something especially sweet about cheerfully cooperating with God when we are not in a crisis. That cooperation (obedience) is seen in outward expressions of a strong love lived out in the dailiness of life's seemingly inconsequential moments (see John 15:14).

4

Think Rightly About the Guide

H ad I been asked a few decades ago if I had an accurate view of God, I would have been fairly confident that my take on God was right. For sure, no one can completely know an infinite God, but I assumed I had a correct big picture of who God was. I cringe now as I admit that my grasp of God was puny and my view of Him skewed.

In my defense, at that point in life, I hadn't been through any significant self-probing, which is often necessary to ferret out one's own convictions about God. My idea of God came from a fusion of biblical facts and my culture. I had not intentionally morphed God into a deity of my own creation, but I also had not been compelled to deeply examine who God was and to know Him.

At the beginning of my raft trip, I knew some details about my guide, but I didn't *know* him. It was only as our group drifted down the river and engaged in conversation, experienced the rapids together, and worked as a team that I got to know my guide better. Spending half a day with him in close proximity expanded my knowledge of him—and helped me think rightly about his level of expertise and his character.

In his book *The Knowledge of the Holy*, A. W. Tozer has an entire chapter on the importance of thinking rightly about God. He wrote, "That our idea of God correspond as nearly as possible to the true being of God is of immense importance to us. . . . Only after an ordeal of painful self-probing are we likely to discover what we actually believe about God. A right conception of God is basic not only to systematic theology but to practical Christian living as well. . . . The man who comes to a right belief about God is relieved of ten thousand temporal problems, for he sees at once that these have to do with matters which at the most cannot concern him for very long."[2]

While it often takes a crisis to drive us to "painful self-probing," we can do the hard work of learning to think rightly about God before the storm, when life is calm and all seems right with the world. Serious followers of Christ don't have the privilege of fashioning a view of God that doesn't align with God as revealed in the Bible. In order to know God—really know Him—we can't create a god that aligns with our culture or personal preferences. Recreating God to fit our desired worldview is modern-day idolatry. In twenty-first-century Western civilization, we don't typically carve wooden idols to worship. We do, however, tend to craft an idea of God that matches our worldviews. Idolatry is serious stuff. God clearly says, "You shall have no other gods before me. You shall not make for yourself an image" (Exod. 20: 3–4). As a Christian, I have no reasonable option but to make every effort to think rightly about God and come to know Him as He has revealed Himself in His Word.

Developing the right concept of God is hard mentally, emotionally, and spiritually, because in so many ways God does not neatly fit into our current culture's worldview of what a god should look like. We tend to project our limited perspective and humanness on God: some view Him as a jolly Santa who doles out requested gifts; others believe that God is aloof and merely sits on His heavenly throne and observes mankind from afar; others have created a god who is nice, fair, and predictable. Yet in God's own words, "When you did these things and I kept silent, you thought I was exactly like you; but I now arraign you and set my accusations before you" (Ps. 50:21). Intentionally or not, those of us who follow Christ often filter our faith and our idea of who God is through our culture, our realities, and our experiences rather than through God's revelation of Himself in the Bible. Tozer continues in *The Knowledge of the Holy*: "The heaviest obligation lying upon the Christian Church today is to purify and elevate her concept of God until it is worthy of Him."[3]

In the months after my husband's death, I was caught off guard as I found myself struggling with seeming inconsistencies between God's character and His actions. Who I had envisioned God to be didn't line up with His actions. Not surprisingly, I quickly realized that my view of God Almighty wasn't accurate, nor was my interpretation of how life should go. I've wondered how different my initial years of widowhood might have been had I sought to know God more intimately and accurately when my husband was alive.

Realizing my deficit in the wake of my loss, I determined to redouble my efforts to know God accurately and intimately. That meant going to the primary source: God's own revelation of Himself in the Bible. I read, studied, and memorized what God has said about Himself. By engaging in the work of intentional and consistent study of the Bible and then prayerfully thinking through what we have studied, the Holy Spirit promises to teach us who diligently seek Him. I call it work because I am not talking about casually reading a five-minute devotion every morning or listening to a podcast while cleaning the kitchen. While I encourage those avenues of exposure to God's Word, genuine relational growth with God through Christ requires the expenditure of dedicated hours of study in the Bible—regularly, over the long haul, year after year. It means scheduling time for digging into the Bible in directed study. It means hours of pondering what we've studied and then wrestling with who God is and who we are in light of who He is.

Almost two thousand years ago, Paul, young Timothy's spiritual mentor, admonished Timothy in a personal letter to concentrate and apply diligent effort to accurately handling the Word of truth (see 2 Tim. 2:15). Words like "diligently" and "accurately" tell us how to interact with the Bible: It is an intentional effort. It doesn't just happen. It's work. The determination to know God and think rightly about who He is should be a lifelong pursuit for us. The reward is "perfect peace" (Isa. 26:3) for those who have exerted the effort, which is a rather amazing benefit to be equipped with for whatever rapids may lie ahead.

5

Appreciate the Guide

would not have characterized myself as an ungrateful person in my pre-widow years, but I also would not have been so generous as to have credited myself with exemplifying a heart of gratitude.

I caught a glimpse of this in myself on my rafting trip. A whitewater rafting guide must embody unique skill sets. He needs to be a people person, able to work with all personality types (from the timid rafter to the showoff). He should have good communication skills, including a voice that can be heard over screams of delight and the noise of rushing water. He must have good upper-body and core strength; no one wants to have a weakling as a raft guide! A working knowledge of basic principles of physics is crucial. Most importantly, a guide must be able to read the river and know how to safely negotiate the technical aspects of white water. Our raft crew flawlessly ran the river primarily because of our guide. He expertly used his paddle as a rudder at the back of the raft to negotiate the dangers, while the rest of us leisurely paddled. Our guide knew the river, he knew the limits and capabilities of the raft, and he undoubtedly knew the skill level of his raft companions after just a few minutes with us as his crew. Our guide made us look good and convinced us that we were quite adept as rafters. Without him we could not have enjoyed that summer day on the river. Yet in retrospect, I realize I didn't express my gratitude to the guide for having successfully (and patiently) negotiated the rapids with a boat full of neophytes.

Today I see gratitude (or the lack thereof) as having an immense impact on shaping my worldview and attitude. When we see life through the lens of gratitude rather than from the constraints of our circumstances, our perspectives go through a metamorphosis. Grateful people acknowledge that what they have has been gifted to them. We are not entitled to anything—not our next breath, not years of marriage, not comfort, not pleasure. Timothy Keller refers to "cosmic ingratitude" that "gives you the delusion that you have the ability to conduct and hold your life together. Actually every day that your heart keeps pumping, your country is not invaded, and your brain keeps functioning is wholly an undeserved gift of God."[4] Okay, based on that definition I did exemplify ingratitude during my married years.

Verbally expressing my gratitude to God regularly in my pre-widow season of life would have meant less wrestling with God over His right to do what He pleased after I became a widow. Thankfulness expressed would have transformed all my attitudes—toward God, myself, others, and life. I did not need ideal circumstances but a transformed heart. In 1633 George Herbert wrote a hymn expressing this universal need for a grateful heart: "Thou that hast given so much to me, / Give one thing more, a grateful heart. . . . / Not thankful when it pleaseth me / As if thy blessings had spare days: / But such a heart whose pulse may be /

Thy praise."[5] Almost four hundred years later, his words inspire me to seek a grateful heart.

I find parallels between my pre-widowhood years and Jesus' encounter with ten lepers on a dusty road in Luke 17. As Jesus walked to Jerusalem, He passed a Samaritan village. On the outskirts of that community, He met ten lepers. The men stood far off. They were required by law to live outside the village, not as punishment or to inflict shame but to stop the spread of the disease. Seeing Jesus, the men lifted up their voices and said, "Jesus, Master, have mercy on us!"

Who knows how many weeks, months, even years these men had been separated from their families? Besides the ravages of the disease, they suffered without the loving care of those dearest to them. When Jesus saw them, He said to them, "Go, show yourselves to the priests." Seems like an odd thing to say to the men. But on examination of the Jewish law (see Lev. 14:1–32), Jesus was actually giving them great news. When a leper appeared to be free of leprosy, he was to go to the priest to be examined and be pronounced disease free. Jesus was telling the ten lepers that they would be healed!

The next verse says "as they went, they were cleansed" (Luke 17:14). Can you imagine the exuberance? The rush to get back to their families? Of course these men hightailed it to the priest—most likely so would you and I, if we were in the same position. But one of the lepers, when he saw that he was healed, returned, and with a loud voice glorified God and fell down on his face at Jesus' feet, giving Him thanks.

I don't think there were ten ungrateful lepers, although that's how I remember it being taught in my Sunday school class as a child. I suspect that all ten lepers were exceedingly grateful for being healed. They had been as much as dead to their families, and now their lives were restored. They were recipients of God's mercy (just what they had asked for)—they got what they didn't deserve but what they desired; they got their lives back. They could return to the arms of those who loved them and resume "normal" life. The significant difference in the one leper who returned to Christ and all the others was that he *verbalized* his gratitude. He *said* to Jesus, "Thank You!"

Cultivating a grateful heart will change our perspective. We are not owed anything; instead, every good thing in our lives is a gift from God. Humbly thanking Him for all He's done shifts our focus from ourselves to Him. What better preparation could there be for the trials of life?

TAKING SPIRITUAL INVENTORY

No matter what season of life we find ourselves in, it is helpful to occasionally pause and give careful thought to our ways. Whether single, married, or widowed, we can establish the discipline of self-examination so we can accurately evaluate our own spiritual lives.

In Ecclesiastes Solomon made a recommendation for preparing for potential challenges in life by acknowledging and honoring God today. His encouragement was to seek God early in life and not wait for a breakdown to turn to the Lord: "Remember your Creator in the days of your youth, before the days of trouble come" (Eccles. 12:1).

It's so easy to bump along from one busy week to another without ever stopping to ponder where we are going and where we should be going. To help bring discipline to this area of my life, I've gathered some probing questions to assist me in the process of reflecting and then making decisions about spiritual disciplines that can refine me as I examine my life. I've split these questions into three parts to coincide with each season discussed in this book. Usually I drag the list out at the beginning of a new year and then review it a few times during the year to see if I'm on track.

Below are some questions to consider in the season of peace and quiet, before significant loss or suffering takes place:

- In which spiritual discipline do you most want to make progress: meeting God for the first time, cooperating with His advance preparation in your life, thinking rightly about Him, or being grateful to Him? What will you do about it?
- How will you incorporate meditation on the character of your Guide in this season of relative peace in your life so as to strengthen your faith for future trials?
- Have you overemphasized any possessions or relationships to the point that they interfere with your relationship with God?
- Have you allowed any of God's blessings to become idols instead of them serving as reminders to you of God's lavish love?
- What single thing do you plan to do this year that will matter most in ten years? In eternity?
- What habit would you most like to establish this year? Why?
- In what area of your life do you most need growth, and what will you do to facilitate that growth?
- What is the most helpful way you could strengthen your marriage this year? Your relationships with other family members? Your relationship with an accountability partner?
- What will you do this year to know God better? To think rightly about God?
- What area of your life most needs simplifying, and what's one thing you could do to begin to make that happen?

PART 2

Plunging into Grief

How I long for the months gone by, for the days when God watched over me,
when his lamp shone on my head and by his light I walked through darkness!
Oh, for the days when I was in my prime, when God's intimate friendship
blessed my house, when the Almighty was still with me
and my children were around me.

JOB 29:1-5

6

Blindsided by Death

t was almost midnight when the headlights shone up the long gravel driveway. "Finally he's home! Why in the world didn't he call to let me know he was going to be so late?" After worrying and wondering for several hours about my husband's delay in returning home, now that his truck lights were shining up the driveway, my worry turned almost instantly to anger. Within seconds, however, fear gripped me. My stomach knotted and my pulse raced as I realized that the vehicle in the driveway wasn't pulling into the normal parking place. The porch light provided enough light for me to see the county sheriff's decal on the side of the vehicle. Two deputies got out of their car and slowly walked to the door.

The news of my husband's death literally took my breath away. I physically struggled for my next breath. I audibly sucked in air—and was startled at the sound of my own gasp. My husband's sudden death was like a ruthless amputation with no anesthetic. The entire landscape of my world changed instantly. Nothing would ever be the same.

In some ways it was a bit like riding the rapids of the Deschutes River. As the afternoon wore on the day of my trip, we negotiated lots of white water—several class II and III rapids. Then our guide let us know that we were coming upon the only class IV rapid of the day: Oak Springs. As we got closer, the water no longer lapped at the sides of the raft but became a churning roar of white foam that yanked the raft up and down. Large boulders of black basalt protruded from the water, shoving the raft into swirling whirlpools that sucked the front of the raft down only to thrust it up and into the air seconds later. Then the river disappeared from under the bow of the raft, and we were plunging down a precipice.

Getting through the rapids took just seconds, but the adrenaline rush lasted for several minutes afterward. So much happened so quickly that it was hard to sort out the sequence of events and what we had just experienced. Drenched and disheveled, my crew members and I mopped our faces and pushed wet hair out of our eyes. We accounted for all the paddles, and some searched fruitlessly for sunglasses. (It does make you wonder how many thousands of pairs of sunglasses sit on the river bottom at the base of the rapids.) Mostly we were just thankful to still be in the raft once the wild ride was over.

Some stretches of a river provide a view of approaching rough water for a significant distance. In other sections, a series of rapids may appear suddenly. Some women have clear signs of the imminent death of their husbands or other loved ones as the ravages of illness take their toll; thoughts of loss occupy their time and emotional energy. Others are suddenly engulfed by the unanticipated separation of death. Either way, the chaos brought on by immeasurable loss can be the tipping point in a woman's spiritual and emotional life.

The weight of my grief, the anguish, the loneliness, the heartache, and the "it's more than I can bear" feeling all cast a heavy cloak of bleakness and pain over my life. It was hard to get my bearings. I couldn't concentrate. Simple tasks were overwhelming. I struggled with my identity as an "amputee." For months tears came at unexpected moments and rendered me nonfunctional. I felt stone cold and empty. My world was engulfed in relentless pain. In the midst of the raw grief, it was impossible for me to think beyond the immediate fog of despondency.

Yet the night my husband died, I knew in my head that God was not capricious. I clearly remember saying out loud to myself, "This accident was not a mistake." I knew that God in His providence had set the date and hour of my husband's death before he was even born (see Ps. 139:16). I believed with all my soul that our days are tenderly held in God's hands. My feelings, however, screamed a dramatically different assessment of my circumstances. Thus began an arduous internal battle between head knowledge and my heart's emotions.

After my husband's death I struggled mightily with God's right to do whatever He wanted with my husband's life, my sons' lives, and my life. I could easily have rattled off ten or twelve attributes of God's character, explained what they meant, and cited reference verses for them. I knew the Sunday school answers. But in many ways all this was information in my head that had not transformed my heart. I was staggered to realize that in the midst of my grief, I was experiencing a faith crisis. Simultaneously I was walking through grief, trying to provide some semblance of normalcy at home for our three sons who were also grieving, and wrestling through my faith. God and I had major work ahead.

7

Acknowledge God's Sovereignty

During this time of incredible pain and searching, my shattered heart was receptive. I ached to understand God and what He was doing in my life. Of course, suffering does not soften everyone's heart; I can't speak for those individuals who pull away from God in their pain. But I was drawn toward God and desperate to understand Him more intimately during my season of suffering. In my brokenness I had new ears to hear. While messy emotions and jumbled thoughts were inextricably knotted together, miraculously it was a time of accelerated spiritual growth.

One thing was very clear to me: God had the absolute right to make decisions that profoundly affected His children—without their permission. I'm stating this in part for myself, because two decades of widowhood have taught me that I continually need to reaffirm Almighty God's independent authority as absolute ruler over every aspect of my life. I suspect I will be learning and relearning this truth until my last breath. But recognizing the sovereignty of God is vital, because it plays profoundly into our ability to spiritually and emotionally survive the turmoil in crisis seasons of life: If God is not sovereign, it doesn't matter how wise or loving He is; He's also powerless. His presence in our daily lives is inconsequential if He is simply a caring but feeble bystander. If He is impotent, His intimate knowledge of us is a moot point.

In the months immediately following my husband's death, Lehman Strauss's book *In God's Waiting Room: Learning Through Suffering* provided me with a working definition of God's sovereignty. Strauss wrote,

> God is the creator and controller of the universe and all that is in it, whether animate or inanimate. Any use or disposition He chooses to make of any part of His creation is His sovereign right. God is accountable only to Himself. He reports to nobody. He is not required at any time to give to any person any explanation for anything He says or does. He is the superpower above all powers in every area of His creation. We do not expect to understand fully the purpose for our trials until our Lord calls us home to be with Him. But we do know that He loves us too much to harm us, and that He is far more concerned with our welfare than we are. God's choices are always right. He is capable of carrying out any project to a successful conclusion without the possibility of fault or failure. Nothing in His universe happens by chance or accident. . . . Yes, God is in control.[1]

As months passed, I went through deep valleys of discouragement and loneliness. I also had fleeting glimpses of hope and joy.

I found genuine encouragement in recognizing that I was not the first person to struggle with questions about God's sovereignty in the midst of crisis. Somehow, knowing that others had gone before me down the same road gave me resolve, even courage.

The book of Job became an anchor for me, as Job expressed so many emotions and questions that I also experienced. I found solace in Job, because he countered the traditional wisdom of his friends with his affirmation that God was just and good even as he wrestled with the difficult question of suffering. Job did not suggest that God was an evil deity or that His power was limited, but he didn't hold back on speaking his mind to God either. Yet in the midst of his anguish, he found words of praise for the Creator's sovereignty, wisdom, and glory.

Over the centuries greater minds than mine have grappled with God's sovereignty and what it means for mankind. A couple questions in the Heidelberg Catechism spoke volumes to me. Question 28 asks, "What advantage is it to us to know that God has created, and by his providence does still uphold all things?" Exactly! While I would never have worded it that way, that was my question: "What good is knowing the right answers about who God is, especially since I don't have corresponding feelings and life is miserable right now? Yeah! What advantage is it?" The catechism's answer:

> That we may be patient in adversity; thankful in prosperity; and that in all things, which may hereafter befall us, we place our firm trust in our faithful God and Father, that nothing shall separate us from his love; since all creatures are so completely in his hand, that without his will they cannot so much as move.

Question 26 in the same catechism asks, "What believest thou when thou sayest, 'I believe in God the Father, Almighty,

Maker of heaven and earth'?" I'd been confessing my belief in
God the Father, Almighty, Maker of heaven and earth for three
decades when my husband died. But now I had to truly examine
what I believed. The catechism's wonderful answer:

> That the eternal Father of our Lord Jesus Christ (who of
> nothing made heaven and earth, with all that is in them;
> who likewise upholds and governs the same by his eternal
> counsel and providence) is for the sake of Christ his Son,
> my God and my Father; on whom I rely so entirely, that I
> have no doubt, but he will provide me with all things nec-
> essary for soul and body and further, that he will make
> whatever evils he sends upon me, in this valley of tears
> turn out to my advantage; for he is able to do it, being
> Almighty God, and willing, being a faithful Father.

I shifted from insisting upon explanations from God to
listening for God. My questions diminished in significance not
because my situation had changed or my questions had been sat-
isfactorily answered but because my picture of God was enlarged
by a developing understanding of His sovereignty. In the midst
of the fray, I began to live in the midst of God's grace.

8

Rebuild Trust in the Guide

During the months immediately following my husband's death, I struggled to trust God. He had allowed what I considered the unthinkable to happen to our family. How could I trust Him going forward? Why should I trust Him? Would it be possible to rebuild my former trust in God? Counting on God as my trustworthy guide took on a whole new meaning.

Plunging over a cliff in a rubber raft was smothering, surreal, overwhelming, all consuming, disorienting. It demanded our team's full attention. The pressure was relentless. The tiny raft seemed at the mercy of the incredible force of water. A foaming wall surged into the raft and engulfed my fellow crew members in front of me. They disappeared in the white spray. My vision suddenly diminished, and I could see only the few feet immediately in front of me. I was unaware of anyone else in the raft and simply hung on for dear life. I think "terror" would be the appropriate word to describe the moment. But while I was unaware that he was doing anything, our guide was still at the back of the raft, expertly maneuvering our raft through the raging water.

Just because my personal situation had radically changed, it did not mean God had. Malachi 3:6 tells us that God does not change. But my shift in circumstances *did* mean that my understanding of God had to be reconstructed. While I was not starting with a blank slate as to who I believed God to be, I had to examine my presuppositions about Him. I needed to scrutinize my previous conclusions about God against the plumb line of His Word in order to form a biblical image of Him and thus genuinely trust the God revealed in the Bible.

The whole process was not a predictable one in which if A = B, then B = C. I'm a slow processor. I spend a lot of time mulling things over; I need time to sort things out. I have always required time to think before I respond and come to conclusions, so I spent months wrestling with God, flipping through the pages of His Word. I tussled back and forth a great deal between my feelings and knowledge.

When rafting a river, it makes no sense to hire an expert guide and not let him fulfill his responsibilities. When a ship's crew loses confidence in the captain of the ship and rebels against his authority, chaos ensues. It's called mutiny, and it rarely results in a positive outcome. Even as I wrestled with trusting God, I grasped the spiritual futility of having a Guide if I questioned His wisdom and doubted His competency.

One of the things I had been trusting in (even though I didn't realize it at the time), my husband, was ripped away from me. So I didn't just suffer the loss of my husband; I also suffered the loss of the identity and security that my relationship to him had provided. During the initial turmoil of my widowhood, the revelation of my mistaken identity and misplaced trust drove me to seriously question my faith. The book *Trusting God* by Jerry Bridges helped me nail down where to find my true identity and what genuine trust in God looked like. In his book Bridges reveals two aspects of trust that are critical to practical living by faith through asking the question "Can I trust God?" The question has to be asked with two different inflections: "Can I *trust* God?" and "Can *I* trust God?"[2]

"Can I *trust* God?" is asking if God has historically proven Himself trustworthy. Is He dependable in times of adversity? Is He worthy of our trust? Are we fully assured that what He has promised, He is able also to perform (see Rom. 4:21)? It's really an academic question. It can be studied historically and grasped intellectually: either God has proven Himself to be trustworthy or He has not. The answer to this question can be logically discerned by intentionally reading the Bible, looking for God's promises, and discovering whether or not He has fulfilled those promises. It can be found by studying the lives of individuals in the Old and New Testaments and seeing how God has worked in their lives for their ultimate good and His glory.

For me, answering the question of God's trustworthiness required a disciplined study of God's revelation of Himself throughout the Bible. Timothy Keller said, "Suffering is a school where students learn things about themselves, about God, and about life that they would never have learned without it. . . . How remarkable that, with the Word of God, a sufferer can come through it all deeper, wiser, richer, more loving, and even happier."[3]

The second question probes the individual's heart: "Can *I* trust God?" It is profoundly personal. It is asking if we can release our white-knuckled grip on our lives and allow God to be our guide. Do we have such a relationship with God and such security in who He is that whether or not we approve of our circumstances, we are confident that He is loving, wise, in control, and with us? Are we able to give up the need to have answers to our "why" questions? Do we believe that He knows better than we do? These are heart questions that require intentional introspection and searching.

No one could answer these questions on my behalf, and satisfactory answers didn't come quickly for me or without significant self-reflection. Answering the question of my personal ability to trust God took me several months. But this was where the theory of my faith and the reality of my faith came together.

In order to trust God, I had to view my adverse circumstances through the eyes of faith, not by what I could see (see 2 Cor. 5:7). I had to resolve both questions "Can I *trust* God?" and "Can *I* trust God?" to be able to experience renewed genuine trust in God. Trusting God was more than giving mental assent to His existence. It was not, do I believe *in* God? but, do I *believe* God?

Daily affirming to Him and reminding myself that He was in charge because of who He is (even when my voice was but a whisper due to lack of confidence) created a footpath for my faith to gradually inch forward. Small steps of faith progressively led to increasing strides. I learned to trust God's heart even when I didn't understand His hand. I learned that trust can be purposefully grown and even rebuilt. Evidence of my faith's growth was often imperceptible in the moment, but it was significant, and the ramifications of my daily decisions to trust God rippled through all aspects of my life.

The rebuilding of my faith in God was one of the most significant things to emerge from the initial turbulent years of my widowhood. I could honestly say, "I cannot, Lord, Thy purpose see, but all is well that's done by Thee."

9

Grieve with Purpose

Grief can't be ignored. It can't be skirted around. It sucks you in.

The sheer force of water rushing over a rocky cliff can fold an inflated raft in half. If the raft gets hung up on a boulder in strong currents, the raft can be pulled underwater and held there with seemingly supernatural power. When I received the news that I was now a widow, the full force of the surging waters of grief slammed into me. It folded me in half and held me in its grip. There is no easing over to the side of the vortex in order to escape the awful impact.

A few months after the death of my husband, friends and acquaintances suggested I should move on with life. They reminded me of Job's friends, who had lots of advice that didn't hit the mark.

In defense of my friends, I was the first among my peers to become a widow. Widowhood was not on any of my friends' radars during this busy stage of life in our forties. This was uncharted ground for every middle-aged friend I had. They were at a loss as to what would be helpful. Consequently, most of them attempted to fix my life and me. They also didn't know that I was not just grieving but also struggling to make sense of my faith. The two experiences were so intertwined that I wasn't able to pull them apart until months later. It is no wonder my friends were at a loss as to how to help me negotiate this season in which God's grace was concealed.

The death of my husband brought me face to face with God's sovereignty as nothing else ever had. It doesn't seem profound to write of it now, but at the time, grasping the truth that life and death were God's to orchestrate changed my perspective on grieving. With my newfound understanding, I resolved that, rather than trying to dodge the pain and anguish I felt, I would fully experience my sorrow and plunge to the depths of my grief. If God had orchestrated the events of my husband's life as well as my own, then I determined to receive them as from my wise, compassionate Father's hand. I would lean into the pain, emotions, and questions. I would fully explore the ache of my loss.

I grieved frequently. I grieved intensely. And five disciplines emerged as beneficial for my emotional health and my spiritual stability during this plunging season: finding time alone with God, identifying and acknowledging my brokenness, giving myself permission to grieve again and again, unloading on God, and finally, rejecting the temptation to feel sorry for myself. Applying these principles was not sequential or a once-and-done experience, and frequently I made a hash of it. But gradually my confusion and pain were transformed into trust and peace. I examine each of these disciplines in the next five chapters.

10

Carve Out Time Alone

Significant loss requires significant time to heal—time to absorb what has happened, to process thoughts and emotions, to search God's Word for insight. Time in and of itself does not heal, but it is an important component in the healing process.

Without apology I gave myself time to grieve deeply and to seek God. Sometimes it was spontaneous. Sometimes it was planned. I found moments in my daily routine or specifically set aside time to work through my heartache before God. It took significant blocks of time to sort through my feelings and thoughts, assimilate my loss and my sons' losses, listen to God, and feed my soul through Scripture. I had much to wrestle with.

Christ demonstrated the necessity of being alone before God. Over and over He pulled away from the frenzied crowds to find solitude with His Father. He encouraged His followers to do the same: "Come away by yourselves to a secluded place and rest a while" (Mark 6:31, NASB). In His greatest hour of anguish, just before His crucifixion, Jesus escaped to an olive grove to find refuge with His Father in prayer. The Gospels tell us that He was distressed, troubled, overwhelmed with sorrow, and deeply grieved, and during that time He was all alone before His Father.

Finding a place to get alone with God as a single parent of three boys wasn't easy for me. Good friends of our family came to my rescue and allowed me to use a quiet apartment tucked away above their office building on their farm as a retreat. They also graciously entertained our youngest son, who was just five when his dad died and not yet in school, so I could escape without distraction. In that apartment I was away from the relentless responsibilities that surrounded me in my home. That upper room was a safe place for rigorous self-examination and quiet time alone with God—time to reflect, cry, pray, study. Over and over I went to that hideaway to be alone with God and slowly heal.

Alone time may seem too melancholy and even frightening for some women. For me it was indispensable for scrutinizing my heart and soul and beginning to understand God's grace and mercy in the midst of my pain and suffering. David's prayer became my prayer: "I call on you, my God, for you will answer me; turn your ear to me and hear my prayer. Show me the wonders of your great love, you who save by your right hand those who take refuge in you. . . . Keep me as the apple of your eye; hide me in the shadow of your wings" (Ps. 17:6–8).

It may be stating the obvious, but plunging into grief cannot be achieved through perpetual busyness. "Some people run away from grief, go on world cruises or move to another town. But they do not escape, I think. The memories, unbidden, spring into their minds, scattered perhaps over years. There is, maybe, something to be said for facing them all deliberately and straightaway."[4]

Constantly filling the day with events and activities or continually being around people as an avoidance tactic does not qualify as plunging into grief either. I have watched other widows work hard at not acknowledging their hurt. Avoidance isn't a long-term solution to pain and grief. At some point getting busy and being surrounded by people become healthy and not just appropriate but necessary. But first a woman must sit alone in the company of God, plunge into her grief, and find her shelter in the shadow of His wings.

11

Face Your Brokenness

I was devastated by the death of my husband. I felt bankrupt. I lost my confidence. I was fractured spiritually and emotionally. I was a mess on the inside. I felt dead. Activities and projects that had previously interested and inspired me now were meaningless and brought no joy. The days dragged on endlessly. Each moment was drudgery.

I was blindsided by my brokenness. What was wrong with me? Weren't Christians supposed to exude hope and peace in the midst of trials? After all, I was an American! Americans pride themselves in their independence, self-sufficiency, competence in the face of insurmountable odds. My mantra as a kid had been "I'd rather do it myself." (Just ask my mom about that attitude!) I was a bootstrap puller-upper. But plunging into grief meant coming to terms with my brokenness, my utter helplessness to resolve my situation, and my inability to recover by myself.

The revamping of my default perspective required time and significant mental wrestling to eventually embrace a biblical worldview of brokenness. Dependence, weakness, and broken-ness were attributes extolled in the Bible, but in my life prior to my loss, I hadn't squared what that looked like lived out. "God wants us broken so that any power in us can be undeniably at-tributed to Him. If self-reliance could reliably and ultimately contribute to our success and fulfillment, God's glory would be diminished . . . . For God to get all the glory, he requires our bro-kenness, while promising his wholeness. He gets the glory when we trust him in difficult times. . . . The cost is high, but so is the benefit."[5]

Most of us don't experience real brokenness until we have had all the supports of our own making knocked out from under us. Our brokenness and weakness simply demonstrate what has been true all along: we are completely dependent on God for life and breath and everything else. That was certainly true for me. Jesus didn't become my absolute treasure until I was out of op-tions. Brokenness was not the end for me but a new beginning, because weakness provided the context in which true strength could be found. Jesus said, "My grace is sufficient for you, for my power is made perfect in weakness," to which Paul responded, "Therefore I will boast all the more gladly about my weaknesses, so that Christ's power may rest on me. That is why, for Christ's sake, I delight in weaknesses . . . in hardships . . . in difficulties. For when I am weak, then I am strong" (2 Cor. 12:9–10). It sounds weird and crazy when we first read it, but it's not. Paul had come to know that God's "power is made perfect" in his weakness. Christ never intended for me to gut my way through life by my own efforts. God made me a frail jar of clay so that He would get the glory when I did experience a victory or modicum of success.

Gradually I realized that weakness was not what I should be afraid of. Rather I should fear the delusion that I was strong. Strong people tend not to reach out for help because they think they don't need it. Only when I had come to the end of my own resources and been proven weak could I tap into the endless resources of divine power that were mine in Christ. If my life was to honestly proclaim the greatness of Christ, it would require me to honestly confess my bankruptcy and then point to Christ, who was the source of strength and courage.

The brokenness unearthed in me when I was thrown into widowhood was a powerful tool God used to expose my self-confidence, self-effort, and self-centeredness. My "strengths" were actually a hindrance to reflecting Christ with my life. Jared Wilson said, "The greater the brokenness, the greater the impulse to trust him. The greater the trust in him, the greater the joy of his salvation. So then, the further to the end of ourselves we go the more of Christ we will enjoy."[6] Brokenness was a vehicle God used in my life so I could more fully experience His grace.

When we experience brokenness, we might feel that God has abandoned us. But the opposite is true. God weeps with us. He is close to the brokenhearted. Psalm 51:17 says, "A broken and contrite heart you, God, will not despise." He has promised to be near to us when we are experiencing brokenness in order to restore and refine us to be more like His Son: "This is what the high and exalted One says—he who lives forever, whose name is holy: 'I live in a high and holy place, but also with the one who is contrite and lowly in spirit, to revive the spirit of the lowly'" (Isa. 57:15). Why is He with the contrite? So that our spirits might be revived. It is amazing that God, who lives forever, who is high and lifted up, longs to reside with us when we are lowly, broken, and unnoticed by society. He wants to lift us up! He wants to restore joy, peace, and contentment to our souls.

Bringing my brokenness to Christ was an arduous process of handing over hidden sins, dashed dreams, an interrupted life, confusion, and all the messiness of me. It meant facing the fact that what my head knew about God and what I had verbally affirmed had not been absorbed into my heart. It required courageously confronting hidden areas of hypocrisy. It entailed confessing the shallowness in my relationship with the author of my life. It was exhausting.

Plunging into my grief entailed an increasingly honest evaluation about my spiritual condition with myself and ultimately with trusted family and friends. As we grapple with our neediness, with God, with regrets, we must admit that we are broken and struggling. We must be honest with ourselves. We must be honest with God. In 1872 Robert Lowry, American pastor and hymnist, candidly wrote, "I need thee every hour, in joy and pain; come quickly and abide or life is vain." Part of plunging into grief is acknowledging our desperate need for God. Brokenness strips away fake spirituality and provides a fresh pallet upon which a vibrant relationship with God, ourselves, family, and friends can develop. In spite of all its pain, brokenness is a manifestation of grace.

12

Grieve Frequently and Repeatedly

My effort to plunge into grief also meant repeatedly grieving. This process of grieving was not something I did once and then checked it off the "How to Grieve Productively" list. My sorrow was not a linear process with a fixed beginning and a defined endpoint. Mourning felt like an unending task, and progress was hard to track.

Grief reared its head frequently during the first two years after my husband's death. Each "first" required its own grieving. I grieved differently as I faced my first wedding anniversary alone than I did upon the arrival of that first Thanksgiving without my husband. Some things I grieved over because of the impact they had on my life at that very moment, and other things I mourned because of their anticipated future impact. I grieved the loss of future conversations with my husband, who had been my spiritual "iron" and had sharpened me. I grieved over the big and little events that my sons would go through without their father and that I would experience alone—events like losing a first tooth, learning to ride a bike, mastering tying a tie, making the all-star team, passing a driver's test, graduating from high school, getting married, getting a master's degree, having grandkids . . . And then there was the grief that swept over me for no perceptible reason. Some sad moments I could anticipate; some were more intense than others; some I shared with other family and friends; some were experienced in solitude.

The ongoing barrage of tears and surges of pain waxed and waned. The time of day (evenings around five o'clock continue to be a melancholy time of day for me), the day of the month (Sunday is the hardest day of my week; it was the day we always spent together as a family), the phase of the moon (every full moon reminds me of the night my husband died), and even the weather (fog is another reminder of the evening of my husband's death) affected me. A new experience, an old experience, a memory, a smell—they all demanded their own time of grieving. After months of grieving and re-grieving and grieving again, I concluded that I didn't need to continually apologize for my tears. (I did usually warn people when I felt tears coming.) Either I would grieve as the moment demanded, or I would have to stuff my sadness and probably struggle for years to come. So no apologies for grieving—again.

Each day brought opportunities to plumb the depths of my grief. As time marched on, I processed my sorrow in shorter chunks of time—it took hours rather than days and eventually minutes rather than hours. Yet even the brief minutes of plunging needed my attention; they were significant slices of life to be processed, sorted through, and laid before Christ.

13

Unload Before God

My plunge into grief included verbally unloading before God. That may sound irreverent. It was not. It was casting (dumping) my cares upon Him (see 1 Pet. 5:6-7) with feeling!

I created a mental picture of myself lugging an oversized backpack to Christ and unceremoniously dropping it at His feet, then turning and walking away. Unloading was really just frank communication with God without denying my emotions. It was moments of "speaking in my heart" (see 1 Sam. 1:13), as Hannah did when she fervently prayed in the house of the Lord in Shiloh. Her prayer was so passionate that the priest who saw her thought she was drunk. Hannah's response to the priest was, "I am a woman who is deeply troubled. I have not been drinking wine or beer; I was pouring out my soul to the LORD. Do not take your servant for a wicked woman; I have been praying here out of my great anguish and grief" (1 Sam. 1:15-16). Hannah's prayer was a desperate prayer as (with no disrespect intended) she unloaded before God.

We see the psalmists unloading on many different occasions throughout the book of Psalms. David said, "I cry aloud to the LORD; I lift up my voice to the LORD for mercy. I pour out before him my complaint; before him I tell my trouble. When my spirit grows faint within me, it is you who watch over my way" (Ps. 142:1–3). David begged God to hear him, care for him, see his desperate need, and rescue him. He unloaded before God, and God honored his honesty.

Neither did Job hold back his complaints (that is Job's word, not mine) against God after a series of devastating losses. He ranted ("ranted" is my word), "I will not keep silent; I will speak out in the anguish of my spirit, I will complain in the bitterness of my soul. . . . I loathe my very life; therefore I will give free reign to my complaint and speak out in the bitterness of my soul. . . . I desire to speak to the Almighty and to argue my case with God" (Job 7:11; 10:1; 13:3). Keep in mind that in the midst of his rant, Job still acknowledged, "Though he slay me, yet will I hope in him" (Job 13:15). He was passionate in his dialog with God but not disrespectful or ignorant of God's absolute authority to be God. He was candid but not crass as he unloaded before God.

Because Christ had gone before me to provide access to the Father, my desperate prayers could be brought before God. "Decorous prayer has its place, but desperate prayer, from the heart, is something that God honors."[7]

John Newton, in the late eighteenth century, expressed the privilege we have as believers to unload before God. He voiced it in eloquent terms in his hymn "Approach, My Soul, the Mercy Seat," which was inspired by Hebrews 4:16: "Let us then approach God's throne of grace with confidence, so that we may receive mercy and find grace to help us in our time of need." John Newton wrote,

Approach my soul, the mercy seat
Where Jesus answers prayer;
There humbly fall before his feet,
For none can perish there.
Thy promise is my only plea;
With this I venture night:
Thou callest burdened souls to Thee
And such, O Lord, am I.[8]

Unloading can get messy, but we can be courageous and verbalize our fears and sorrows. It's okay to say them out loud and helpful to write them down. God can handle our sorrows, our doubts, and our fears. As our Creator, He knows our limits and limitations. As our Father, He cares about us. God weeps with us (see John 11:35). He understands (see Ps. 103:13–14). He *knows* the heaviness of our hearts. Healing can occur in the process of putting words to our deep-rooted feelings and taking them to God.

14

Refuse Self-Pity

The fifth and final lesson I learned to apply when I plunged into grief was to refuse to indulge in self-pity. Lonely women seem especially susceptible to self-pity. I have watched other widows cling to the role of a victim for years after their husbands have died. ("I've been hurt; I've been wronged; I have the right to be bitter, and you should feel sorry for me.") But mostly I base it on my own proclivity to feel sorry for myself and wallow in elaborate "poor me" scenarios. In a fairly short time, I was able to convince myself that no one had experienced sorrow such as I in those years immediately after my husband's death.

My self-pity was exposed when I realized that I was repeatedly rehearsing (in silent conversations with myself) all the reasons I had to feel sorry for myself and could legitimately expect others to pity me also. My internal conversations with others went something like this: *Do you realize I am the youngest widow around? There are other women who have been married longer than I've even been alive! And now I've been invited to attend the widow's Bible study with women who are twice my age. I'd need to get a babysitter to attend. People seem oblivious to my real needs. Things might have been easier to handle had there been some warning, but a plane accident? So suddenly? He left one morning for work, and that was our last good-bye! And seriously, can you think of a worse time of the year to have your husband suddenly die than three days before Christmas? And our sons—three boys who need their dad. Am I supposed to fill the shoes of both parents now? Not to mention I've got no family within 150 miles! And, and, and . . .*

When I was engrossed in my world of self-pity, I developed tunnel vision and attempted to create a case against the character of God. He obviously was not in control! He was impotent, or He would have intervened! He was unkind and unjust! He was a fraud! If ever there was an exercise in futility, my hours spent in self-pity were one. My sessions of self-pity were not just unproductive and not reflective of reality; they were sin—sin that required confession.

Oswald Chambers used the term "dejection" for the idea of self-induced misery and had little tolerance for the habit: "Dejection is a sign of sickness. . . . Dejection spiritually is wrong, and we are always to blame for it."[9] Once I admitted that indulging in self-pity was not just counterproductive but also wrong, I needed to replace my distorted thinking with right thinking. Thinking rightly about who God was began to transform my tendency toward self-pity into settled acceptance of and contentment with my lot in life.

Contentment was not the fulfillment of what I wanted but the realization of how much I already had. Contentment meant not wavering from believing what God had promised in His Word as absolutely true and that He was able to accomplish what He had said He would do (see Rom. 4:21). The promise that He knew the plans He had for my life and that those plans were to give me a future and a hope (see Jer. 29:11) helped me reframe my circumstances. Assurance that everything He had woven into my life would work toward my ultimate good (see Rom. 8:28) and His glory also gave me a broader understanding of my life than just the moment I was living in. Because God's essential nature is goodness and love, I knew that He always did what was best for His children.

Developing the habit of contentment meant accepting that God, who is all wise, knew better than I what I needed. He was entirely capable of bringing to pass what He had promised and was indeed in control, and I needed to be okay with that.

Contentment was an attitude I had to choose. It's the same in all spiritual battles—we have to choose God's way. I'll admit that there were brief moments when I "enjoyed" wallowing in self-pity, but the enjoyment did not satisfy for long. It always took me to a dark place. I had to be ruthless with myself, take myself by the scruff of the neck and refuse to listen to my own "poor me" self-talk. Instead, a self-lecture on the attributes of God was in order.

I'm not a quick learner, but eventually I figured out that contentment was impossible unless my eyes were kept on my heavenly Father. Isaiah 26:3 was a great reminder that God would give me perfect peace as I kept my mind focused on Him. "There is nothing which more surely indicates we have already succumbed to the wiles of the Devil than to complain about what happens to us. The Word of God invariably points out that the mark of a Christian who has learned how to be a Christian is that he rejoices in everything, gives thanks in all things."[10] Perfect peace and self-pity don't live in the same moment.

We must not allow ourselves to linger over the dark pit of victimization. Self-pity wallpapers our minds with unhealthy and inaccurate views of our realities. It distorts our views of God. The longer the wallpaper is up, the more we come to believe it to be an accurate representation of our lives and of God.

Ultimately, plunging into our grief is not work we can delegate to someone else. We have to spend a lot of time face to face with God across life's conference table in order to emerge from our grief able to live out emotionally healthy lives and reflect Christ daily in our years ahead. Paul reminded the Philippian church to do all things without grumbling or complaining so that they would become children of God who shone like stars in the universe (see Phil. 2:15). As remarkable as it may seem today, not in spite of loss but because of it God can make us like stars in the universe for His glory.

15

Discover Purpose in the Turmoil

As the immediate shock of my widowhood diminished, I desperately wanted to make sense of my pain and loss. What was the purpose of all the anguish? I operated under the assumption that I could discern the mind of God regarding my catastrophic life change. (Not a great assumption, but that was where I was emotionally.) I was plagued by the question of why. One of the things that made the death of my husband so difficult for me spiritually was the myriad of unanswered theological questions that refused to allow me rest. I felt isolated from people because they didn't understand what I was experiencing. I was confused and exhausted. Increasingly, my loss seemed pointless. My whys bounced back with no response from God.

One day while reading my Bible, I came across a verse in the book of Proverbs that said "it is the glory of God to conceal a matter" (Prov. 25:2). This was not what I wanted to hear. I don't like surprises, and I don't appreciate information intentionally being withheld from me either, especially when it comes to things that shake my world. I wanted explanations from God, not concealment.

Wrongly I presumed that I was able and entitled to know what God was doing because He was doing it to me. I had several flaws in my thinking at this point. Maybe most importantly, I had overlooked Christ's work on my behalf—I had been bought with a price and was no longer my own (see 1 Cor. 6:19–20). I was not the owner of my life; I was the steward. I slowly realized that my real beef was with God acting like God! God, in His infinite love and wisdom, had chosen not to answer all my questions—and that was His prerogative. As the sovereign ruler of the universe, He did not have to account for any of His actions to me or anyone.

Despite its painful mysteries, suffering does have a purpose in our lives. The rapids in a river likewise serve a beneficial purpose in the entire ecosystem's health. God in His wisdom has littered His mountain streams and rivers with rocks and logs. As water tumbles over rocks in a riverbed, the splashing pulls oxygen into the water and creates a river filled with tiny bubbles infused with oxygen, a vital element for life. The oxygen-saturated water can then sustain a myriad of aquatic plants and animals. Even the nearby land ecosystems benefit from the splashing water of the river.

In God's grace and perfect timing, He gave me insight into the purpose of my suffering. My sister-in-law loaned me some videotapes of a presentation by Elisabeth Elliot titled *Suffering Is Not for Nothing*. Elisabeth Elliot became a widow in 1956 when her husband was killed by the people group in Ecuador they were trying to share the gospel with. Their daughter was ten months old when her father was speared to death in the jungle by Auca Indians. Elisabeth Elliot's teaching immediately gained credibility with me, and her message revolutionized my thinking about suffering. Through her presentation I realized that not only *could* there be purpose in suffering, but also that there *is* purpose in suffering. This purpose was grander than I could envision at that time in my life.

Through suffering God does one of two things: He either *restores* us, giving us back what we have lost, or He *redeems* our suffering. Often He weaves together restoration and redemption like two threads in a breathtaking tapestry.

My dictionary defines restoration as "the act of bringing back to a former, original, or normal condition; returning to a state of health, soundness, or vigor; putting back to a former place."[11] God Almighty restored Job after the loss of all his wealth and the death of his children: "The LORD blessed the latter part of Job's life more than the former part. He had fourteen thousand sheep, six thousand camels, a thousand yoke of oxen and a thousand donkeys. And he also had seven sons and three daughters. . . . Nowhere in all the land were there found women as beautiful as Job's daughters, and their father granted them an inheritance along with their brothers" (Job 42:12–15).

When God redeems our suffering, on the other hand, He exchanges or amends our temporal suffering with treasures of eternal value. At the time of my husband's death, you couldn't have convinced me that it would be possible for God to restore *or* redeem my suffering. But gradually I came to see that He was redeeming my loss, in part, by enabling me to experience His grace in the midst of life's suffering. Trusting God when I couldn't see what He was doing has produced the sweetest fellowship I have ever had with Him. God uses human suffering to accomplish transformation in us and bring glory to Himself.

"The pain of life is subject to his power and prerogatives. Because of this—because our heavenly Father who is not just loving but love itself is in control over all that befalls us—we can be confident that our pain is being used for our good. We can be sure that no thorns will pierce our flesh except those that will do so for his glory."[12] Elisabeth Elliot said, "It is through the deepest suffering that God has taught me the deepest lessons. And if we'll trust Him for it, we can come to the unshakeable assurance that He is in charge, He has a loving purpose, and He can transform something terrible into something wonderful. Suffering is never for nothing."[13]

The emotional pain of widowhood played a necessary and significant role in deepening my faith. Ascribing positive value to suffering was a major worldview shift for me. I had to redefine the word "good." It no longer meant happy, convenient, enjoyable. I shifted to thinking of "good" as things with eternal positive significance rather than temporal pleasure. Nurturing a long view of life helped temper my need to know why and to have life fixed immediately.

Something else that helped me through this season of life was acknowledging that suffering was a common experience to mankind. "The Bible doesn't pull any punches. At every turn, it informs and warns us about the nature of the world. Scripture works to prepare us, not so we will live in fear, but so we will be ready for the things we will face. God gives us everything we need so that we will live with realistic expectations and so moments of difficulty will not be full of shock, fear, and panic, but experienced with faith, calm, and confident choices."[14]

Jesus said, "In this world you will have trouble" (John 16:33). Hundreds of years before that, the psalmist said, "You have put me in the lowest pit, in the darkest depths. . . . You have overwhelmed me with all your waves. You have taken from me my closest friends. . . . Why, LORD, do you reject me and hide your face from me? . . . You have taken from me friend and neighbor—darkness is my closest friend" (Ps. 88:6–18).

Job asked the Lord a plethora of questions after the death of all his children, the loss of his worldly wealth, and the deterioration of his physical health. He struggled with the same questions that plagued me—questions of why. Yet with hope and a long view of life, he said, "If I go to the east, [God] is not there; if I go to the west, I do not find him. When he is at work in the north, I do not see him, when he turns to the south, I catch no glimpse of him. But he knows the way that I take; when he has tested me, I will come forth as gold" (Job 23:8-10). When the Lord finally responded to Job, He didn't answer the questions Job had posed; instead God revealed Himself to Job through penetrating questions of His own. Job's suffering had purpose. His unanswered questions did not change God's sovereignty, goodness, or wisdom. In spite of receiving no direct answers, Job did acknowledge that his suffering was not for nothing.

Over thousands of years of biblical history, I traced a thread of mankind suffering and experiencing pain in this broken world. That is a lot of people who have travailed in anguish and with whom I had a bond of suffering and loss. It seems strange and a bit morose, but it was helpful for me to know that I had not been singled out. I was not alone in my suffering.

God concealing matters from His children is His absolute right. He doesn't have to answer for His actions to anyone—not even those whose lives are impacted. As I grasped the reality that God intended to do something much loftier in my suffering than just answer my "why" questions, I accepted the pain itself as purposeful. "There is design in the suffering we experience. There are a great many things we can do nothing about, but that we can do something with."[15] My grief, my pain, my unanswered questions were all ways for God to draw me to Himself and grow my relationship with Him as nothing else could. I found comfort in knowing that our heavenly Father, who does not change and makes no mistakes, was directing and using the suffering that crossed my life's path.

Suffering is purposeful in our lives. It is used for our good and God's glory, whether or not we ever know the why. No matter what vehicle God uses to accomplish His plan, our suffering has purpose. Everything that happens fits into a pattern for good.

16

Paddle Through the Rapids

When we get into white water, we are going to dig in those paddles and paddle hard," our guide told us. "I want you to keep paddling through the rapids. Don't stop paddling until I tell you to stop."

Had he just said, "Paddle through the rapids"? Up until then I had thought all our guide's instructions had sounded intuitive and almost unnecessary, but this "paddle through the rapids" thing struck me as odd and uncalled for. If we were already clipping along at breakneck speed, why would we want to keep paddling and increase our speed? I wondered if our guide just wanted to give us a bigger thrill so we would feel as if we'd gotten our money's worth by careening as fast as possible through the cascading water.

But I was to learn that strong, consistent paddling actually gives a raft stability in turbulent water. While we didn't know what was ahead, our guide did, and he knew how to best negotiate the rapids ahead. He also knew that our first few miles of practice paddling down the peaceful river had actually been preparation for the rapids ahead, when paddling would be important for stability. Once we reached the section of the river with a series of successive rapids, the opportunity to apply what we had been learning was before us. So in deference to our guide's instruction, we kept doing what we had been doing: we paddled.

Trying new techniques as a boat teeters on the brink of cascading water is an unwise rafting strategy. That same principle applies to surviving the first turbulent years of widowhood. Life does not stop; it is necessary to keep moving forward. Maintaining already-established routines gives life stability when so much has changed.

Balanced, logical thinking was not a hallmark of this turbulent season of my life. Concentration was difficult at best. I lacked the emotional energy to establish new disciplines. I had to be reliant upon my normal routine because so much of me was absorbed in the grief process. In my grieving I defaulted to well-established habits—things that didn't require decisions to be made in order to be executed. I simply did the next thing that needed to be done. I didn't do a lot of advance planning. If the laundry needed to be done, I did the laundry. That was about as much planning as I was capable of.

I gleaned the principle of "doing the next thing" from Elisabeth Elliot, who credited an anonymous ancient English poem for the idea. The poem admonished the believer to confidently respond to life's daily challenges with prayer and reverence, "tracing His Hand / Who placed it before thee with / Earnest command. Stayed on Omnipotence / Safe 'neath His wing / Leave all resultings, / Do the next thing."[16]

I am so grateful that God in His goodness poked and prodded me in my teen years to make a daily quiet time with Him a priority. Daily Bible study was a non-negotiable. Because it had been my habit to have a regular time of Bible study and prayer each morning, in my early widowhood I kept doing that. I did it out of habit—I didn't have to make a decision to do it. I had also regularly walked my neighborhood for exercise, so I kept on walking my neighborhood. I continued to putter in the garden. And three boys still needed to be fed, so I cooked their meals. I just kept paddling, usually crying as I did so. I did the next thing.

For most women a barrage of decisions comes with significant loss or suffering—decisions not previously required of them. The responsibility of making so many decisions, even insignificant ones, can be daunting. Grieving can paralyze us. We can't concentrate, so we find ourselves relying upon our daily routines.

The routines we have developed over time will either positively or negatively impact our journeys through grief. If we have intentionally invested in our own spiritual well-being during the calm waters of life, nurturing habits that will support an unshakeable faith through life's difficult seasons, then these disciplines will be the *petra* that anchor us through times of turmoil, tears, exhaustion, loneliness, and pain. Then "do the next thing" can become the mantra that will move us through the dailiness of life. We should not give ourselves permission to check out of life at this point. We can plod on by doing the next thing. It doesn't have to be a big thing, just the next small step.

TAKING SPIRITUAL INVENTORY

As we noted at the end of part 1, our faith needs regular checkups to improve our spiritual lives and help us avoid (or at least minimize) faith crises. At one point in the Old Testament, when the people of God had become careless in their relationship with Him and lax in their dedication to His commands, the Lord called them out through Haggai His prophet: "Give careful thought to your ways" (Hag. 1:5). Haggai urged the people to reflect on events happening to them as a nation and individually, and to evaluate their slipshod spirituality in light of what they knew of God and His commands.

Give some consideration to these questions as you navigate the early season of loss:

- What is the most important decision you must face in this new season of life? Can you break it into small steps and "do the next thing"?
- What is one healthy way that you will intentionally plunge into your grief this year: carving out time alone, facing your brokenness, grieving often and repeatedly, unloading before God, or refusing self-pity?

- What is the most humanly impossible thing you will ask God to do?
- How will you incorporate meditation on the character of the Guide in this season so as to strengthen your faith for this season of suffering?
- What is something you could do to increase your enjoyment of God?
- What is a significant way that you will, by God's grace, try to make this season of life count for eternity?
- What is one thing you can do to grow your trust in God this year?
- What is one thing you regret that you didn't say or do while your loved one was alive, and what will you do about it in this season?

PART 3

Embracing
Abundant Life

*Praise be to the God and Father of our Lord Jesus Christ, the Father of
compassion and the God of all comfort, who comforts us in all our troubles,
so that we can comfort those in any trouble with the comfort we ourselves have
received from God. For just as we share abundantly in the sufferings of Christ,
so also our comfort abounds through Christ.*

1 CORINTHIANS 1:3-5

17

A New Assignment

Two or three years after the death of my husband, I realized that I was moving out of the deep, profound grief of the months immediately surrounding his death. I didn't wake up one day and recognize that I was at a pivotal point in my grief process; rather my understanding of what was happening slowly unfolded. Gradually I discovered moments of joy and a sense of purpose in life again. I had fewer unexpected meltdowns. My emotions were not as fragile as they had been a few months before. I was pleasantly surprised when periodically I genuinely looked forward to doing something.

"There is a time for everything, and a season for every activity under the heavens: a time to be born and a time to die, . . . a time to weep and a time to laugh, a time to mourn and a time to dance" (Eccles. 3:1–4). In the fullness of time following a deep loss, God imparts to us new perspectives, new responsibilities, and new purpose.

On the third anniversary of my husband's death, I sent this letter to close friends and family members:

One morning you wake up and realize *it* isn't the first thing you think of. That single thought is a landmark in the long grieving process. There is a lightness to the soul, an inner rejoicing that a weight is slowly lifting. Then following the first realization of the change is the sickening thought that you have somehow betrayed the one you loved. The wrestling with changing emotions, changing roles, and changing thoughts is mental commotion. I cringe to have to deal with yet another change in my emotional response life.

All this unsought-after change means the me of 2002 is quite different from the me prior to December 1999. After having the privilege of sitting in on one session of my son's college sophomore philosophy class during parents' weekend last May, I have thought a lot about the topic of the class discussion: "What is the essence of me?" If I lose a leg, become blind, gain weight, have a heart transplant, color my hair . . . am I still me? What is the unchangeable part of me that makes me, me? We probably would all agree that the outward, visible me isn't the essence of me. So what happens when a person is changed inwardly through life's experiences? What becomes of the original me as new, previously unknown parts of me develop? How much change can happen before a person is no longer the original me? Leon Bloy said, "Man has places in his heart which do not yet exist, and into them He [God] enters suffering in order that they may have existence." Those places that didn't previously exist are not more me than the original me. They are the enhanced me.

Not long ago I got my hair cut, and a few people commented, "Oh, I see you changed your hairstyle." (I'm never sure how to respond to such a statement.) I'm sure they were just making small talk, but my thought was, *You think my hair has changed? You should see the inside of me.* The deep changes in a person make it hard for friends to know how to react to the person and often create awkward relationships. It is hard to "just be you" when even you aren't sure who you are.

The changing essence of me is both cause of excitement and cause for sorrow. I liked my life prior to Roger's death. I was not seeking a change. I saw my happy, secure home as a gift from God. Yet now I also see the changes in me as a work of God's. In some way or other, we will all have to learn the difference between trusting in the good gifts of God and trusting in the good Giver. The gift may be good for a while, but the Giver is the eternal Good.

Since this non-traditional letter is my Christmas greeting, I will pray that you might come to welcome the unexpected changes God brings into your life this coming year. While much in life changes, He does not change (Mal. 3:6). By our estimations He is often an intruder into our comfortable life. If you acknowledge Him as your creator and Lord, the reality is that He can't intrude into what He owns. It is His sovereign privilege to do what pleases Him.

During this time of transition, it became evident to me that I was a different person. I had been changed by virtue of the experience of widowhood. I recognized profound shifts in my spiritual walk with Christ. I had never undergone such sustained, intimate communion with Christ as I did after the death of my husband. I had resolved the "Can *I* trust God?" question. My expanded understanding of God's sovereignty had resulted in less anxiety and worry. My hard work of grieving and of wrestling with difficult theological questions had produced unexpected spiritual fruit. I had personally experienced God's mercy and grace, and He was continuing to refine me.

I had also changed as I shouldered additional family responsibilities. Being the sole parent of three boys had been daunting, especially since they too had been altered by the death of their father. I had tried to learn what it was like to grieve as a boy. I had sought counsel to understand how children at different ages process grief and deal with relational voids in their lives. I had taken on the role of spiritual leader in the house, which had at times been challenged by those very boys I loved so dearly and desperately wanted to draw near to God in spite of their own pain and questions. I had learned the rules of water polo, baseball, and golf so I could converse with my sons with some degree of knowledge about what was an important part of their lives. I had struggled to teach them what it meant to respect their mother when that was a job their father had done with conviction and wisdom. And some days I had just struggled. But all the changes and new responsibilities had refined us as a family and me personally. Life would be different forever, and I found myself standing at the edge of a new phase of life.

What God permits, He permits for a reason. I slowly realized that I would waste my widowhood if I did not believe it was designed for me by God. In my married years it had been natural for me to acknowledge good things as gifts from God (see James 1:17). But receiving "bad" things brought into my life as a test from His hand required a different level of trust. "Shall we accept good from God, and not trouble?" (Job 2:10). This unique period of life was like pulling away from the turbulence of the rapids and evaluating life based on the recent experience of going through the white water, then looking forward and asking who

I would be for the rest of my journey as I pushed back out into the current.

Now, as a not-so-newish widow, I saw a new assignment waiting for me. I had decisions to make. Would my fear of what was next have such a grip on me that it would paralyze me from living abundantly? Would I remain focused on my loss and what might have been? Or would I purpose to thrive in my new assignment from God? Would I accept this new role as from the Father's hand?

It is not ours to know how many days we have left or the details of God's long-range plan for us. But we do have a choice as to how we spend those days. God has assured us of His presence, provision, and protection. After the death of her husband, Oswald, Biddy Chambers said, "Future plans are uncertain, but we all know that there is first God's Plan to be lived, and we can safely leave everything to Him, 'carefully careless' of it all."[1] Christ often calls those who have mourned to special assignments in His kingdom. We need to stay in the boat with our Guide and embrace the rest of the journey.

18

Be There for Others

'm not a trained counselor. I'm not an expert on grief. I don't
have an educational background in human behavior. But I do
have a little insight into some of the challenges a widow who
is clinging to her faith faces. I know what profound sorrow feels
like. And by virtue of that experience, God has asked me time and
again to be there for others who are walking through consider-
able loss of their own.

Once our raft crew had careened through the rapids, our
guide wasted no time providing us with new instructions. While
the immediate challenge of getting through the rapids was behind us, the water was anything but calm at the base of the rapids. Paddles in hand, we worked our way downstream a hundred
feet or so at our guide's directions and headed toward the bank
of the river. Maneuvering our way out of the current to an eddy
(referred to as a parking spot on the river), we regrouped. We
high-fived each other, gave ourselves kudos for staying in the raft,

and exclaimed over and over how amazing it had been. "What's next?" we asked.

"Well, we're going to hang here for a little bit," our guide told us. "I like to wait for the next raft to come through the rapids before we continue on down the river. We're going to make sure they don't need any extra help once they're through the rough water."

Suddenly this raft trip became something more than just an adventure for me to recount to my friends. We were delaying our journey in order to be there for people we didn't know just in case they needed a hand. We were now first responders for the other novice rafters on the river. We were in a strategic position to help.

The wait was not long. Another raft teetered briefly at the top of the boiling spillway and then plunged down the churning waters of Oak Springs. Hearing the rafters' screams and seeing their raft fold in half as the bow hit the white water at the base of the rapids gave me renewed respect for the extraordinary force of the water. The raft we were watching had started out with eight people in it; not all of them had negotiated the rapids in the raft. Paddles and people bobbed downstream.

With one fluid motion, our guide threw out a mesh rescue bag with a rope coiled in it. As the bag flew through the air, the rope slithered out. The guide's toss had sent the rescue line directly downriver of an adrift rafter; she grabbed the rope as the current pushed her into it. With a group effort, our crew pulled her to the side of our boat, hoisted her into the raft with us, and then shoved off to rescue the rogue paddles that continued floating downstream. With paddles eventually rounded up and on board, we headed to the riverbank to transfer our additional passenger back to her own raft, which had also pulled out of the main current by this time.

Looking back to that day on the Deschutes River, this event was the pinnacle of the raft trip for me. When we first pulled over, our guide didn't know if our help would be needed, but his years of experience had given him insight into the challenges of negotiating the rapids and the likelihood that others would need help. His thoughtfulness underscored the importance he placed on our boatful of rafters contributing to the success of other rafters. Temporarily we set aside our plans in order to be there for people we didn't even know, people who might need a little help after coming through the roiling water. Because we had negotiated the rapids just a few minutes earlier, our crew was now both available and in possession of a basic knowledge of what going through a set of class IV rapids was like. We weren't experienced first responders, but at that moment, on that day, we were the "men" for the job.

Since the death of my husband, I've had scores of such moments when I've gotten to be part of the rescue mission for others who have come along behind me. Long before Esther became queen of Persia, God was preparing, molding, and equipping her for future service to accomplish His plan. Then, in the fullness of His time, God strategically placed her in a calculated role where she could be used by Him "for such a time as this" (Esther 4:14). It wasn't a fluke that she found herself in a position of influence and power at that pivotal point in her nation's history. She had been groomed and prepped for that moment by God Himself, and some of her preparation had included sorrow, hardship, and anxiety.

Finding ourselves in the right place at the right time is like red flashing lights and blaring sirens saying, "The providence of God made visible to you!" Life's "coincidences" are observable indications of God's hand orchestrating the details of our lives. God places and equips His children uniquely so they can extend His compassion, love, and grace to those within their sphere of influence for such a time as this. Paul reminds us that we are comforted by God not just because we need comfort but so we can then turn around and be the conduit God uses to comfort someone else (see 2 Cor. 1:4). Few things are more humbling and, at the same time, more satisfying than being able to be there for someone in the midst of that person's need. A bond develops between those who have been broken by grief. The path of grief is a powerful connection that can knit believers together and become a rescue line to help pull someone to safety. As believers, we are able to comfort one another with the comfort with which we ourselves have been comforted.

The woman with a few years of sorrow under her belt can be a valuable resource to a woman who isn't as far along in her new life assignment. Being there for the next grieving person is a privilege, but it is also a charge. It is more than just an opportunity; it is actually a responsibility. Paul instructs us, "We who are strong ought to bear the weaknesses of those without strength and not just please ourselves" (Rom. 15:1, NASB), and, "Carry each other's burdens, and in this way you will fulfill the law of Christ" (Gal. 6:2). He also reminded the Christians in Corinth, "Stand firm. Let nothing move you. Always give yourselves fully to the work of the Lord, because you know that your labor in the Lord is not in vain" (1 Cor. 15:58).

Authentic ministry responsibilities aren't always planned, scheduled, or convenient. By definition, a responsibility is a burden of obligation upon the one who is answerable or accountable for the task.[2] This role of being there for someone else is a serious assignment from God that shouldn't be considered optional. We have to set aside our personal plans in order to fulfill God's assignment. What we have suffered through, experienced, and learned are gifts from God; they are not ours to hoard. The new insights I gained into God's character through my early years of widowhood, my heightened empathy and compassion, and my bolstered confidence in Christ's faithfulness are all priceless treasures. I am to invest them freely and share them with others. It is a privilege to be the instrument God uses to provide comfort and hope in the moments when others need it most.

My new life assignment has been saturated with "for such a time as this" encounters. These appointments have been given to me not so much for myself but for those who come behind me and need a glimpse into the mercies and wisdom of God. My task is to pull out of life's current for a bit, position myself to see those around me who may be floundering, and then be there for them. God is gracious to use those who are available to further His kingdom for His glory and our good.

19

Reengage with Life

n my initial years of widowhood, my need for extended alone time with God was intense. Now, as I reengaged with life, my emotional and social needs changed. I was slow to recognize these changing needs—my default mode had been solitude in many areas of life for so long. But in this new stretch of my widowhood journey, it became important for me to move my focus beyond myself and my sons. This shift didn't begin to occur on a specific date. I realized gradually that I needed to intentionally reengage with my community.

Once a raft has made it through the rapids and had some time to regroup, at some point the crew must decide to push off into the river again and complete the course. The raft can't stay in the quiet eddy forever; there is an unfinished course ahead. After our rescue mission, we did a little reorganizing and proceeded back into the main current of the river. The rest of the trip had some lovely calm water with springs bubbling down the side of the canyon and into the river. We even stopped for a few minutes to enjoy a brief walk along a section of sandy river bank where wildflowers grew. Then it was back in the raft for one last class III rapid before we pulled out for the day just above Shearer Falls.

For an introvert like me, pushing out from the safety of my solitude was an awkward stretch. I certainly found it more comfortable to be a hermit. I recognized, however, that extended periods of isolation didn't lend themselves to my seeing life accurately. I had developed tunnel vision and begun to think it was all about me. I struggled to keep a balanced perspective and even found myself getting defensive when I perceived people were encroaching on my time and space. I had perfected the art of dodging questions on intimate personal topics so as to protect myself.

But when my caring friends began to irritate me, I knew that the issue was with me, not them. The signs of unhealthy isolation and introspection were pretty evident to me, and I had a heart-to-heart talk with myself regarding how to live a life that honored Christ and brought glory to Him. Proverbs' stern words, "A man who isolates himself seeks his own desire" (Prov. 18:1, NKJV), reprimanded me and pushed me to acknowledge my self-centeredness. I knew I had to reconnect with my friends, my community, and my church. Thankfully, I had friends who had stuck with me through all the messiness of the past few years and were there for me.

Fifty-nine verses in the New Testament contain the phrase "one another" in them. We are instructed to love one another, comfort one another, forgive one another, care for one another, build up one another, be kind to one another, live in harmony with one another, accept one another, be patient with one another, teach one another . . . None of these instructions can be done while cloistered. As a widow with a few years' experience, I had much to offer others; conversely, my friends and family had much to offer me. That meant that I had to interact with people on a deep, inclusive level. I had to be willing to take risks in relationships, be vulnerable, and honestly share myself. I needed to see people as having intrinsic value because they were created in God's image. They were God's prized possessions. I was not to see people as interruptions or inconveniences to be avoided.

We are not rugged individuals called to live in isolation from one another. We are created for relationship, so withdrawing from people means losing touch with God's plan for healthy community and any sort of meaningful ministry. Neither withholding myself nor rejecting others resembled a life well lived. God had uniquely equipped me for this season of life, and I was compelled not to waste my widowhood.

Another aspect of reengaging for me was to do something just plain fun. It was easy for life to get heavy under the burden of my obligations. My sons would probably concur that I wasn't nearly as lighthearted of a person as I had been when I was just Mom and not Mom and Dad. I had become a bit of a stick in the mud under the weight of perpetual responsibility. Even now, years after my husband's death, a dark cloud often hangs over me if I work hard for days without some enjoyable outlet.

Day hikes became my fun reengagement activity. I am blessed to live between the Cascade and Ochoco Mountains. Within an hour's drive either east or west, I can be at a trailhead, hike four or five hours, and be back home after another hour's drive. As I reconnected with life, refreshing my soul in God's creation, breathing in the mountain air, and exerting myself physically all revived me. Life came into perspective while standing on the summit of a ridge and taking in a spectacular panoramic view. The hours of hiking also provided extended opportunities for me to ponder life and pray. I came home from my hikes tired in body but refreshed in spirit.

It is important to make an effort to engage regularly in rewarding activities that enrich our lives and the lives of others. It could be volunteering at the library, playing golf, joining a book club, gardening, horseback riding, reading to grade-school kids, serving at a community food kitchen, volunteering for a non-profit organization—really, the sky's the limit. We can and should be creative and give ourselves permission to enjoy life again.

Sorrow is a terrible thing to waste. When we decide to protect ourselves and withdraw from people and life, everyone loses. We must not allow ourselves to hole up and check out of relationships and events. Instead, we can genuinely embrace the incredible assignment that God gives us in our seasons of loss.

20

Accept Help Graciously

As a young widow, I was immediately surrounded by friends and family the first few weeks after the death of my husband, and their help was invaluable. They moved in as first responders and rescued me. I needed them. My sons needed them. It was like the rafter who fell out of her boat when going over the rapids—she was more than happy to be rescued by total strangers who had marginal rescue skills. All her pride had gone rushing downstream with the current, and any help was welcome. My own need was so immense and intense in the early stage of my widowhood that pride did not interfere with accepting people's help.

As months turned into years, however, the type of help I needed changed just as my grieving changed. Certainly I no longer needed friends to bring us meals. (Meals are sort of the Christian community's default response to grief.) I didn't need nightly phone calls asking how I was doing. However, I did need help knowing whether that new squeak the car was making was serious or if it could be ignored. I needed mature Christian men to invest in my sons' lives. I needed recommendations on whether it was time to have the house reroofed. I needed investment advice. I needed substantive adult interaction. I needed friends who were comfortable listening to me talk about my loss yet again.

Yet all the while it became harder for me to graciously accept help. Even in the middle of my neediness, the ugly, boney fingers of pride gripped me and gave the enemy access to yet another area of my life. Satan is ruthless and will take advantage of any opportunity to deceive and taint our faith. He is especially proficient at attacking us when we are already down. He is no respecter of those who are hurting. The needy are prime targets. And target me he did.

My pride kept me from asking for help when I genuinely needed it. My pride made me critical of help when it was offered. People providing help didn't do it the way my husband would have if he had been there. Friends provided "help" in areas in which I hadn't requested assistance and didn't need assistance. (I was not appreciative. I was not gracious. I didn't like being needy. It was not a pretty time in my life.) While friends and family struggled to know how to support me, I struggled with pride and trying to prove to myself and others that I could handle all the new responsibilities that had fallen into my lap as a result of widowhood.

Well, the reality was, I was only one person. I couldn't keep up with the relentless responsibilities. Not only did I strain under the workload, but I also had a hard time admitting that I was incapable of handling the multitude of tasks. I didn't like feeling inadequate. I didn't like needing people. Today it seems ridiculous, but pride is deceptive, and I didn't see then what I can now. I needed to come to the place at which I could graciously accept help and let go of my pride.

God was also aware of my genuine needs. Actually, He knew more than I what I needed, and more than once He sent someone to help me at just the right moment.

About five months after my husband's death, a neighbor I really didn't know knocked on my door and said, "I'm sorry to bother you. I really don't know why I'm here other than the Holy Spirit wouldn't let me drive past your home one more time without stopping." I unceremoniously broke down sobbing as I invited her in. (At this point I'm sure she was wondering what she had gotten herself into.) I explained that it was my son's sixth birthday and a few of his friends were to come over for a small birthday party in a few hours and I had been genuinely non-functional all morning. How could I possibly pull it together to have a birthday party when I had been crying since I had gotten up? How could I celebrate my son's first birthday without his dad? I couldn't imagine even singing "happy" birthday.

God knew my hurt, saw my need, and sent an unlikely neighbor to remind me of His faithfulness and His care for me. She stayed only a few minutes. She prayed with me and gave me a hug. She didn't "fix" anything. She was God's special messenger at that moment for me. I was humbled to think that God cared so much for me that He would direct another believer to set aside her plans for a few moments and step into my world of pain. Over the years I have thought of her sensitivity to the leading of the Lord and thanked Him multiple times for her obedience and kindness.

Timothy Keller prayed, "Let thankfulness begin to transform all my attitudes, toward You [God], myself, others and life."[3] My journey of widowhood going forward was now to be characterized by gratitude. Gratitude to God and my family and the many friends who genuinely cared about me. Gratitude whether or not it was help I wanted or help I needed.

21

Don't Compare Your Loss

Loss is a singular experience for each woman. God's distribution of suffering is not equal, and as such, no two people experience grief the same way.

The characteristics of Oak Springs rapids change seasonally, because the Deschutes River's water source is largely snowmelt from the Cascade Mountains. During the summer the alpine snow melts drop by drop and trickles into babbling streams; then it joins rushing creeks and eventually makes its way into the powerful Deschutes River. The Deschutes (from French, *rivière des chutes*, "river of the falls") is named for the distinct chutes, or channels, in its black basalt riverbed. When water levels are high, boulders normally visible in late summer become hidden under torrents of white water. Conditions such as the volume of water, turbidity, temperature, and speed of the river vary throughout the year. Even wind conditions can influence the rapids' behavior.

Additionally, the amount of gear on board a raft, the number of people in the raft, and the occupants' weight distribution all affect how the raft rides in the water. With so many variables, each passage is a unique story.

When a follower of Christ who is fresh in her faith experiences devastating loss, she will not process it in the same way a seasoned Christian would. When a person endures suffering and pain due to injustice, it will involve complications not experienced by the sufferer whose personhood remains intact. The death of an infant elicits questions that are not asked by someone grieving a loved one who has lived a long and full life. Loss that is a result of an individual's own sin results in both guilt and grief simultaneously. Indeed, in each of these scenarios, the person struggling faces loss and grief, but her story is distinct, and not unexpectedly, her grief is as well.

The events that surrounded my husband's death meant that what I felt, thought, and prayed about did not look like any other woman's grief walk. Consequently, what provided solace for me might not be meaningful to another woman. Scripture that powerfully spoke to me might not resonate with another mourner. Just as each woman is individually handcrafted by God, so too each loss and grief experience is distinctive.

Even while I have acknowledged this truth to myself, I have easily slipped at times into comparing my loss with others. And without much effort, I have convinced myself that my loss was sadder than that of all others and my grief more significant. Over the years I've seen that I'm not the only one who has struggled with this. Did I want pity, so I was rehearsing how devastating my life was? Was my identity wrapped up in my loss rather than in my Savior? Did I find some twisted satisfaction in one-upping another widow? My messy game of comparison revealed that I saw myself as a victim. The "Whose Loss Is Greatest?" contest has its roots inextricably entangled in false martyrdom.

As a child, my mother referred to this sort of behavior as being a "rytram" (pronounced RIT-ram), which is the word "martyr" spelled backward. It is ugly and does nothing to further the kingdom of God. When comparing my loss to another person's loss, I unintentionally turned my husband's death into a tool for the enemy's destructive purposes. So I called a truce. I determined that I would not waste my time trying to convince others (or myself) that I had suffered as none other. Bereavement and loss should bind sufferers together rather than pit them against each other.

My determination to stop being a "rytram" didn't mean the temptation to compare my grief to others' disappeared. But having identified the beast, I was able to take a stance against it. When thoughts of comparison crept in, I reminded myself that I needed to speak truth to myself rather than listen to the enemy's lies. The fact that I was a steward of my life, my time, my resources became a conversation I had with myself multiple times. My goal was to be a steward worthy of the gifts I had been entrusted with. That meant I had to nip the tendency to compare in the bud.

Lots of rough edges in my character have been exposed because of the suffering and questioning of widowhood—rough edges that I might not have been aware of without being a widow, rough edges that need to be chipped away. There was a season for grieving and plunging into loss, but there was also a time to accept my new assignment and to do it with grace, gratitude, and without comparing.

22

Proclaim the Guide's Faithfulness

What a missed opportunity if I fail to use my widowhood story as an occasion to witness to the greatness of Christ!

I certainly spoke highly of my river guide upon returning from my rafting trip. Our guide was great—so much so that I raved to friends about how fantastic he was. Throughout the trip he oversaw our group's safety. He took care of logistics. He put our needs above his own. He considered each of us worth the investment of his time and energy, and not because we brought remarkable skills to the excursion. We recognized (and he knew) that he was both the brawn and the brains of the operation. We knew that we could depend upon him to complete the journey with us. He was worth his weight in gold!

My story is really a story about Christ's adequacy, mercy, and grace extended to me in a season of chaos and grief. It is Christ's story, because He who is in me is greater than he who is in the world. In the midst of the fray, Christ has been ever present with me. God has been faithful day in and day out in profound public ways and in the private minutiae that have made up my life.

David said, "I do not hide your righteousness in my heart; I speak of your faithfulness and your saving help. I do not conceal your love and your faithfulness from the great assembly" (Ps. 40:10). Just a few sentences after this declaration, David asked the Lord to make haste to help him and deliver him from those who sought to destroy his life. David is a remarkable example for me, because even in the midst of his trials, he still practiced reciting God's faithfulness and love.

In the sixth century BC, Jeremiah, the weeping prophet, wrote words acclaiming God's faithfulness amid Israel's sorrow and grief. The nation had been invaded, God's people had been carried into captivity, and Jerusalem was destroyed and desolate. Yet Jeremiah declared, "I remember my affliction and my wandering, the bitterness and the gall. I well remember them, and my soul is downcast within me. Yet this I call to mind and therefore I have hope: Because of the LORD's great love we are not consumed, for his compassions never fail. They are new every morning; great is your faithfulness" (Lam. 3:19–23).

As a widow, I have much to testify about regarding God's mercy, wisdom, love, patience, and sovereignty. Anyone who has walked through tragedy and seen God's hand in the process does. We have the street credentials to speak volumes about God's provision as few other people do. With each new day God reveals His faithfulness to us. Sharing our personal stories of God's faithfulness with those who come after us is powerful. People who look at our lives and see how God has been faithful to us can't help but be impacted by God's goodness in the challenges of loss.

Those who have been through the rapids can offer real encouragement and hope to those who are facing the rapids. What an opportunity to attest to the many benefits God has poured out—benefits that can only be attributed to Him.

23

Plus Ultra—
Go Further Beyond

oss does not represent a mark in the sand indicating that dynamic service for Christ should now halt. Rather it is a new set of orders, a new assignment—an assignment for which a woman previously was not equipped but now uniquely can fulfill.

Recently I came across the Latin phrase *plus ultra* ("further beyond"). It's the present-day motto for the country of Spain. It's on their country's flag and has been emblazoned on their coins over the centuries. But originally it was stated in the negative (*non plus ultra*).

According to Greek mythology, *non plus ultra* ("nothing further beyond") was engraved on the Pillars of Hercules near the Straits of Gibraltar to caution sailors not to venture beyond the final boundary of the then-known world. Beyond the pillars were the Atlantic Ocean and, as far as the ancient mariners knew, the edge of the world. *Non plus ultra* served as a warning to sailors and navigators to go no further.

But according to legend, the warning was changed to an inspirational challenge in the early sixteenth century by Luigi Marliano, an advisor for young King Charles V of Spain (1500-1558). Marliano dropped the negative from the phrase, and *plus ultra* became Charles's motto. *Plus ultra* was used to expand the young king's idea of what was possible and to challenge the ancient superstitions. Charles was encouraged to take risks and go "further beyond." Under his rule Spain's territories expanded significantly. Charles brought under Spanish rule large chunks of land in Europe, including the Netherlands, parts of Austria, and the German states. Across the Atlantic Hernán Cortés conquered Mexico (1519-1521), and Francisco Pizarro overcame the Incas of Peru (1532-1533). Between 1519 and 1522, five Spanish ships under the leadership of the Portuguese captain Fernando Magellan became the first to circumnavigate the globe.

Five centuries later and across the Atlantic Ocean, *plus ultra* rings true today for women who wholly desire to walk with God through the remaining years of their lives. I don't want to under-live the final years of my life on Earth. While I don't know specifically what the "further beyond" may entail, I am convinced that God has more beyond for those He has invested so much into through His grace. We have more lives to touch with God's compassion, more minds to challenge through God's Word, and more hearts to encourage with genuine hope.

TAKING SPIRITUAL INVENTORY

As we have already discussed, we must be intentional and take time to evaluate our lives, make plans, set goals, and live with biblical diligence, remembering that "the plans of the diligent lead surely to advantage" (Prov. 21:5, NASB).

Consider the following questions for the season of embracing abundant life. The value of these questions is not in their profundity but in the simple fact that they bring an issue or commitment into focus.

- What one person will you determine to be there for this year?
- Who do you most want to encourage in this season of life?
- How will you actively reengage with your church family this year? Your community? (Maybe even your own family?)
- What project, issue, or challenge do you need help with in this season of life? Who could be a trusted resource to help you with this?
- How will you incorporate meditation on the character of the Guide into this season so as to strengthen your faith for future trials?

- What is the most important need you feel burdened to meet this year?
- In what spiritual discipline—being there for others, reengaging with life, accepting help graciously, not comparing your loss, proclaiming God's faithfulness, or going further beyond—do you most want to make progress, and what will you do to grow in that area?
- What is one thing you can do to enrich the spiritual legacy you will leave to your children and grandchildren?
- To what one person who has cared for you will you express your gratitude?
- What book, in addition to the Bible, do you want to read in order to increase your vision for a *plus ultra* future?
- What skill do you most want to learn or improve this year?
- To what need or ministry will you try to invest yourself in this season?

CONCLUSION

Facing Forward

Today finds me living alone. I have not remarried, much to the chagrin of a handful of my friends who have given matchmaking their best efforts. I eat most of my meals alone. I work in my garden alone. I do my shopping alone. I go to church alone. I usually hike alone. If I attend a social function, it is usually alone. Those are simply statements of fact and not intended to solicit sympathy.

But truly I am not alone. One of the priceless gifts I have as a believer in Christ is the continual, intimate presence of the Holy Spirit (see Rom. 8:11). While I may be physically alone, I'm not alone, because God as the Holy Spirit is always with me. Not only do I continually have His presence, but He also intercedes, guides, directs, instructs, corrects, and encourages me. The Holy Spirit is engaged with me every moment of every day.

No matter our circumstances today, all of us can imagine something better for ourselves. But God always writes a better story for us than we could write for ourselves. Better doesn't mean easy, pleasant, or pain free. Better is based on this: God Himself is the best, most satisfying thing we could ever have or experience, and therefore fullness of life is ultimately found not in any earthly success, relationship, or accomplishment but in our proximity to God through faith.

Whether we have experienced great loss or not, "we are all caught temporarily in a little drop of sadness here on earth. But eventually it will be removed. Regardless of what happens immediately to believers, eventually it will be all right."[1] This world's story began with our eternal Father speaking into creation the heavens and the earth, and it was good (see Gen. 1). It will end with a new beginning characterized by restoration, renewal, reconciliation, and regeneration, and it will be good as well. Eventually things will be restored to the original perfect relational harmony God established in the garden of Eden. We will finally get to experience genuine *shalom*—"the webbing together of God, humans, and all creation in justice, fulfillment, and delight."[2] God will make His home with His people. The final chapter of our eternal story is summarized in the words of Jesus Himself: "Look! God's dwelling place is now among the people, and he will dwell with them. They will be his people, and God himself will be with them and be their God. He will wipe every tear from their eyes. There will be no more death or mourning or crying or pain, for the old order of things has passed away. . . . I am making everything new!" (Rev. 21:3–5).

For now we are visitors here on Earth; this temporal existence is not meant to be home. It is not our *real* home. During World War II, C.S. Lewis described the believer's existence as "living in a part of the universe occupied by the rebel. Enemy-occupied territory—that is what this world is."[3] But soon we will experience the ultimate *plus ultra*—our heavenly home with the rightful Ruler reigning and the redeemed enjoying the restoration of the fullness of their relationship with God. Lewis summarizes the promised future of the Christian: "Firstly, that we shall be in Christ; secondly, that we shall be like Him; thirdly, with an enormous wealth of imagery, that we shall have 'glory'; fourthly, that we shall, in some sense, be fed or feasted or entertained; and, finally, that we shall have some sort of official position in the universe—ruling cities, judging angels, being pillars of God's temple."[4]

Too often my focus is on this temporal physical world around me and my existence in this specific point in time. I forget to lift my head and see the larger eternal destiny that is mine in Christ: perfect restoration. There is indeed more beyond this life. It is almost too good to be true—I have been created to live forever, and the forever is in perfect wholeness. It is beyond my ability to comprehend. But all followers of Christ will enjoy universal flourishing, perfect harmony, joyful wonder, and fruitful employment—shalom, the way things are supposed to be.

So "we do not lose heart. Though outwardly we are wasting away, yet inwardly we are being renewed day by day. For our light and momentary troubles are achieving for us an eternal glory that far outweighs them all. So we fix our eyes not on what is seen, but on what is unseen, since what is seen is temporary, but what is unseen is eternal" (2 Cor. 4:16–18).

As followers of Christ, we know that the best is yet to be. One glad day we shall lay down our cumbersome loads, shed the fetters that restrict us, and see Him face to face. Until then we can choose to live life on this earth facing forward, as Henry Van Dyke aspired to in the poem he wrote:

Let me but live my life from year to year,
With forward face and unreluctant soul;
Not hurrying to, nor turning from the goal;
Not mourning for the things that disappear
In the dim past, nor holding back in fear
From what the future veils.[5]

I "pray that you'll live well for the Master, making him proud of you as you work hard in his orchard. As you learn more and more how God works, you will learn how to do *your* work. [I] pray that you'll have the strength to stick it out over the long haul—not the grim strength of gritting your teeth but the glory-strength God gives. It is strength that endures the unendurable and spills over into joy, thanking the Father who makes us strong enough to take part in everything bright and beautiful that he has for us" (Col. 1:10–12, MSG). And always facing forward.

NOTES

Introduction: Candid Conversation

. Diana B. Elliott and Tavia Simmons, *Marital Events of Americans: 2009,* US Census Bureau, August 2011, https://www.census.gov/library/publications/2011/acs/acs-13.html (accessed October 19, 2018).
2. "Marital Status of the U.S. Population in 2017, by Sex, in Millions," *Statista,* https://www.statista.com/statistics/242030/marital-status-of-the-us-population-by-sex/ (accessed October 19, 2018).
3. "Widowhood—Demography of the Widowed," Marriage and Family Encyclopedia, http://family.jrank.org/pages/1753/Widowhood-Demography-Widowed.html (accessed October 19, 2018).
4. "Suicide Rates Rising Across the U.S.," Centers for Disease Control and Prevention, June 7, 2018, https://www.cdc.gov/media/releases/2018/p0607-suicide-prevention.html (accessed December 10, 2018).
5. "Motor Vehicle Crash Death," Centers for Disease Control and Prevention, July 18, 2016, https://www.cdc.gov/vitalsigns/motor-vehicle-safety/index.html (accessed December 10, 2018).
6. "Mortality in the United States," Centers for Disease Control and Prevention, December 2017, https://www.cdc.gov/nchs/products/databriefs/db293.htm (accessed December 10, 2018).
7. *Webster's Encyclopedic Unabridged Dictionary of the English Language* (New York: Random, 1996), s.v. "Selah."
8. Heidelberg Catechism, Westminster Theological Seminary, https://students.wts.edu/resources/creeds/heidelberg.html (accessed October 19, 2018).
9. "Safety Code of American Whitewater," American Whitewater, https://www.americanwhitewater.org/content/Wiki/safety:start (accessed October 19, 2018).

Part 1: Preparing for Loss

1. Charles R. Swindoll, *Growing Strong in the Seasons of Life* (Grand Rapids: Zondervan, 1994), 61.
2. A. W. Tozer, *The Knowledge of the Holy* (San Francisco: Harper & Row, 1961), 2.
3. Ibid., 4.
4. Timothy Keller, *The Songs of Jesus: A Year of Daily Devotions in the Psalms* (New York: Viking, 2015), 273.
5. George Herbert, "Gratefulness," in John Tobin, ed., *George Herbert: The Complete English Poems* (London: Penguin, 2005), 115.

Part 2: Plunging into Grief

1. Lehman Strauss, *In God's Waiting Room: Learning Through Suffering* (Chicago: Moody, 1985), 18.
2. Jerry Bridges, *Trusting God: Even When Life Hurts* (Colorado Springs: NavPress, 1988), 16.

27

3. Keller, *The Songs of Jesus*, 312.
4. Sheldon Vanauken, *A Severe Mercy: A Story of Faith, Tragedy, and Triumph* (San Francisco: Harper & Row, 1977), 194–95.
5. Jared C. Wilson, *Gospel Wakefulness* (Wheaton: Crossway, 2011), 40.
6. Ibid., 41.
7. Keller, *The Songs of Jesus*, 353.
8. John Newton, "Approach, My Soul, the Mercy Seat" in *Trinity Hymnal* (Suwanee, GA: Great Commission Publications, 1990), 507.
9. Oswald Chambers, *My Utmost for His Highest* (New York: Dodd, Mead & Co., 1935), February 7.
10. Ray C. Stedman, *Spiritual Warfare: How to Stand Firm in the Faith* (Waco: Word, 1976), 81.
11. *Webster's*, s.v. "Restoration."
12. Wilson, *Gospel Wakefulness*, 46.
13. Elisabeth Elliot, "The Terrible Truth," *Suffering Is Not for Nothing*, video series, Ligonier, 1989, https://www.ligonier.org/blog/suffering-not-nothing-teaching-series-elisabeth-elliot/ (accessed December 20, 2018).
14. Paul David Tripp, "How Suffering Reveals Your True Self," Core Christianity, November 26, 2018, https://corechristianity.com/resource-library/articles/how-suffering-reveals-your-true-self (accessed December 10, 2018).
15. Elliot, *Suffering Is Not for Nothing*, video series.
16. "Do the Next Thing," A Christian Home, http://www.achristianhome.org/Good_Things/a_poem_quoted_by_elisabeth_elliot.htm (accessed December 10, 2018).

Part 3: Embracing Abundant Life
1. Biddy Chambers in David McCasland, *Oswald Chambers: Abandoned to God* (Grand Rapids: Discovery House, 1993), 276.
2. *Webster's*, s.v. "Responsibility."
3. Keller, *The Songs of Jesus*, 356.

Conclusion: Facing Forward
1. Keller, *The Songs of Jesus*, 122.
2. Cornelius Plantinga Jr., "Sin: Not the Way It's Supposed to Be," https://henrycenter.tiu.edu/wp-content/uploads/2014/01/Cornelius-Plantinga_Sin.pdf (accessed December 10, 2018).
3. C. S. Lewis, *Mere Christianity* (New York: Harper One, 1980), 45–46.
4. Lewis, *The Weight of Glory and Other Addresses* (Grand Rapids: Eerdmans, 1949), 7.
5. Henry Van Dyke, "Life," public domain.

32362981R00072

Made in the USA
Lexington, KY
01 March 2019